CORPORATE
SPIN-OFFS

New Titles from QUORUM BOOKS

CORPORATE SPIN-OFFS

Strategy for the 1980s

RONALD J. KUDLA
AND
THOMAS H. McINISH

Q

QUORUM BOOKS

WESTPORT, CONNECTICUT • LONDON, ENGLAND

Copyright Acknowledgments

The following have generously given permission to use materials taken from copyrighted works:

AT & T Shareowners Newsletter, Fourth Quarter 1982. Extracts reprinted with permission.

"The Sum of the Parts . . . ," January 14, 1981. Oppenheimer & Co., Inc. Extracts reprinted with permission.

"Valuation Consequences of Corporate Spin-Offs," *Review of Business and Economic Research,* March 1983: 71-77. Extracts, Tables 1-3 and Figure 1 reprinted with permission.

Chapter 7, figure and table, reprinted from "The Microeconomic Consequences of an Involuntary Corporate Spin-Off," by Ronald J. Kudla and Thomas H. McInish, *Sloan Management Review,* Vol. 22, No. 4, pp. 41-5, by permission of the publisher. Copyright © 1981 by the Sloan Management Review Association. All rights reserved.

Figure 8.1. Winch Truck Providing Wireline Services, Reproduced by permission of Gearhart Industries, Inc.

Appendix D reprinted by permission of Royce B. McKinley, President, Santa Anita Realty Enterprises, Inc.

Library of Congress Cataloging in Publication Data

Kudla, Ronald J.
  Corporate spin-offs.

  Bibliography: p.
  Includes index.
  1. Corporate divestiture—United States.
I. McInish, Thomas H. II. Title.
HD2746.6.K82 1984   658.1'6   83-13705
ISBN 0-89930-030-8 (lib. bdg.)

Library of Congress Catalog Card Number: 83-13705
ISBN: 0-89930-030-8

First published in 1984 by Quorum Books

Greenwood Press
A division of Congressional Information Service, Inc.
88 Post Road West, Westport, Connecticut 06881

Printed in the United States of America

10 9 8 7 6 5 4 3 2 1

To Mary, Hilary, Allison, and Thomas Kudla
and
To Mary Brown

Contents

Figures

Tables

CORPORATE SPIN-OFFS

Introduction

1

In this book the term "corporate spin-off" is defined as the distribution of all or substantially all of the ownership interest of one firm (the parent) in another firm (the subsidiary) to the parent's shareholders so that following the spin-off there are two separate publicly held companies. This type of divestiture is in contrast to divestitures in general where the divested company is completely absorbed by another firm. In addition, the parent firm does not receive any funds (and incurs expenses) in connection with the spin-off.

In contrast to the intense merger activity of the 1960s, the decade of the 1970s was characterized by a growing number of divestitures and spin-offs.[1] According to Hayes (1972) the divestitures of the 1970s were a "natural aftermath of the merger fever of the 1960's." The merger activity in the 1960s was motivated primarily by the desire for diversification.

But in the 1970s, with high rates of inflation and interest rates, management attention shifted to a focus on the best utilization of the firm's assets. Corporate executives began to realize that some business segments were diverting resources from other business segments that were more profitable and where management had greater managerial and technical competence. Thus companies turned increasingly to divestitures and spin-offs as "asset redeployment strategies" designed to streamline operations, increase profitability and market value, and reduce risk.

The corporate spin-off trend accelerated in the 1970s. Table 1.1 gives a partial list of corporate spin-offs that occurred during the last decade.

Table 1.1
A Partial List of Corporate Spin-Offs, 1968-1982

Parent Firm	Spun-Off Firm	Date of Spin-Off*
American Natural Resources Co.	Primark Corporation	Jan. 1982
Peabody International Corporation	GEO International Corporation	Jan. 1981
Cellu-Craft, Inc.	Central Services Ind., Inc.	Jan. 1981
Mid-American Petroleum, Inc.	Mid-American Drilling and Exploration Inc.	Jan. 1981
Dillingham Corporation	Ala Mohna Hawaii Properties	July 1981
Calny, Inc.	Taco Charley, Inc.	Oct. 1981
Central Louisiana Energy Corporation	Central Louisiana Electric Co., Inc.	Nov. 1981
Standex International Corporation	Bingo King Company, Inc.	Nov. 1981
TSC Corporation	Sippican Ocean Systems Inc.	Nov. 1981
	Aviation Simulation Technology, Inc.	Nov. 1981
Imperial Corporation of America	Gibraltar Savings Association	Dec. 1981
Coastal States Gas Corporation	Valero Energy Corporation	Jan. 1980
Alaska Airlines, Inc.	Alaska Northwest Properties, Inc.	Feb. 1980
J. B. Ivey & Co.	Ivey Properties, Inc.	Mar. 1980
Safeguard Industries, Inc.	Delta Queen Steamboat Co.	
The Coca-Cola Bottling Co. of New York, Inc.		Apr. 1980
	Safeguard Business Systems, Inc.	Mar. 1980
MGM Grand Hotels, Inc.	Metro-Goldwyn Mayer Film Co.	June 1980
Hotel Investors Trust	Hotel Investors Corp.	June 1980
The Coastal Corporation	Coastal International, Ltd.	Sept. 1980
Koger Properties, Inc.	The Koger Company	Oct. 1980
American Financial Corporation	Provident Bancorp, Inc.	Oct. 1980
Archer-Daniel Midland Co.	National City Bancorp.	Oct. 1980
Fuqua Industries, Inc.	Interstate Motor Freight System	Oct. 1980
Texas American Resources, Inc.	Republic Resources Inc.	Nov. 1980
Olix Industries, Inc.	Cramer, Inc.	Dec. 1980

* Ex-dividend date, i.e., the date after which purchasers of shares in the parent would not receive shares in the spun-off firm. The ex-dividend date will normally differ from the announcement date, the date the spin-off was approved by the board of directors and the actual date of the distribution.

Table 1.1 *(continued)*
A Partial List of Corporate Spin-Offs, 1968-1982

Parent Firm	Spun-Off Firm	Date of Spin-Off*
Trans Union Corporation	International Shipholding Corporation	Apr. 1979
Tandycrafts Inc.	Color Tile, Inc.	Apr. 1979
Reliance Group Incorporated	Leasco Corporation	May 1979
Sperry and Hutchinson Co.	State National Bancorp, Inc.	May 1979
Centronics Data Computer Corp.	Gamex Industries, Inc.	May 1979
American Agronomics Corporation	Coastland Corporation of Florida	June 1979
EIP Microwave, Inc.	Cushman Electronics, Inc.	Sept. 1979
Mesa Petroleum Co.	Mesa Royalty Trust	Nov. 1979
IU International Corporation	Gotaas-Larsen Shipping Corporation	Dec. 1979
Santa Anita Consolidated, Inc.	Santa Anita Operating Co. Santa Anita Realty Enterprises, Inc.	Dec. 1979
Dynell Electronics Corp.	Solid Photography, Inc.	Feb. 1978
Cole National Corp.	Cole Consumer Products, Inc.	Mar. 1978
Gearhart-Owen Industries, Inc.	Pengo Industries, Inc.	June 1978
Brenner Industries, Inc.	Brenner Companies, Inc.	Sept. 1978
Parsons Corp.	RMP International, Ltd.	Sept. 1978
OSR Corp.	Osrow Products Corp.	Oct. 1978
Pioneer Western Corp.	Pioneer Group Inc.	Nov. 1978
Tyler Corporation	Coronus Industries, Inc.	Apr. 1977
Rorer Group, Inc.	Amchem Products, Inc.	Apr. 1977
Corco, Inc.	Liqui-Box Corp.	May 1977
Logistics Industries Corporation	Checkpoint Systems, Inc.	June 1977
Oxford Industries, Inc.	Lanier Business Products, Inc.	July 1977
Rossmoor Corp.	Laguna Hills Utility Co. Rossmoor Construction Corp.	Oct. 1977
Bendix Corporation	Facet Enterprises, Inc.	Mar. 1976
Tandycrafts, Inc.	Stafford-Lowdon, Inc.	Apr. 1976
Sea Containers, Inc.	Sea Containers Atlantic, Inc.	June 1976
Kingstip, Inc.	Kingstip Communications, Inc.	July 1976
Browning-Ferris Industries, Inc.	Consolidated Fibres, Inc.	Oct. 1976
Refac Technology Development Corp.	Scriptomatic, Inc.	Dec. 1976
The L. E. Myers Co.	The L. E. Myers Co. International, Ltd.	Dec. 1976

5

Table 1.1 *(continued)*
A Partial List of Corporate Spin-Offs, 1968-1982

Parent Firm	Spun-Off Firm	Date of Spin-Off*
Thermo National Industries, Inc.	Republic Metal Products, Inc.	Jan. 1975
Versa/Technologies Inc.	Stearns Manufacturing Co.	Mar. 1975
Turner Communications Corp.	Turner Advertising Co.	May 1975
Southdown, Inc.	Vachi, Inc.	May 1975
Harvest Industries Inc.	Harvest Recreation Vehicles Inc.	May 1975
Ilex Corp.	Compu-Serv Network, Inc.	June 1975
Tandy Corp.	Tandycrafts, Inc.	Oct. 1975
	Tandy Brands, Inc.	Oct. 1975
Woods Corp.	Woods Petroleum Corp.	Dec. 1975
Weco Development Corp.	Citrus County Land Bureau, Inc.	Dec. 1975
Standard Prudential Corp.	Yuba Goldfield, Inc.	Apr. 1974
Olin Corporation	Olinkraft, Inc.	May 1974
TIF Instruments, Inc.	Miami Airconditioning Co.	June 1974
First Union Equity & Mortgage Investors	First Union Inc.	Dec. 1974
Consurgico Corp.	Southeastern Surgical Supply Co., Inc.	May 1973
Stem Industries, Inc.	Stem Development Corp.	June 1973
Gray Communications Systems, Inc.	Gray Cablevision, Inc.	June 1973
Valmac Industries, Inc.	Distribuco, Inc.	July 1973
Industrial Resources, Inc.	Utah Land and Minerals Corp.	Nov. 1973
IPM Technology, Inc.	Electrical Precision Meter Co., Inc.	Aug. 1972
Easco Corp.	Eastmet Corp.	Nov. 1972
Georgia-Pacific Corporation	Louisiana Pacific Corp.	Dec. 1972
Cannon Craft Co.	Cannon Craft Western Co.	Jan. 1971
Obit Instrument Corp.	Ginberg & Co.	Mar. 1971
CBS Inc.	Viacom International Inc.	June 1971
Nestlé-Lemur Co.	Smith, Miller & Patch, Inc.	Mar. 1970
Major Pool Equipment Corp.	Continental Plastics and Chemical	Sept. 1968

Much of the data for this book is based on a careful analysis of the annual reports, registration statements, proxy statements, and other material from these firms.

The purpose of this book is to provide information to corporate executives which may be useful in evaluating the suitability of a spin-off as a part of their strategic plan. In addition, the book serves as a reference for executives actually involved in spin-offs. While there is a wealth of literature available on mergers, surprisingly little information is available on corporate spin-offs.[2] During the preparation of this book a number of senior executives who had been responsible for managing a spin-off commented on the dearth of information concerning spin-offs.

As more executives become familiar with the spin-off strategy and learn the benefits of this strategy as described in this book, an increase in the number of spin-offs can be expected. Few other tools can be used to achieve such a wide variety of corporate objectives. In a complex and rapidly changing business environment characterized by increased competition and regulation, the spin-off is a tool which managers cannot ignore.

Corporate spin-offs can be voluntary or involuntary. Voluntary spin-offs are expected to provide benefits to stockholders of the parent firm. While many divestitures are motivated by the desire to dispose of unprofitable operations, corporations which are spun off are more likely to be financially healthy. There are many very good business reasons for spinning off highly profitable operating units or subsidiaries. These are explained in detail in Chapter 2.

Involuntary spin-offs may result from a variety of causes. Commonly, involuntary spin-offs are the result of complaints filed by a federal or state regulatory agency. Federal complaints filed by the Federal Trade Commission or the Department of Justice usually allege violation of antitrust laws, especially Section 7 of the Clayton Act which prohibits the acquisition of the stock of a competing firm if the effect of the acquisition is substantially to reduce competition. Under the act, previously consummated acquisitions can be the subject of divestiture orders. An involuntary spin-off may be used as a way to accomplish the separation of one operating entity from another.

At the time this book was being written (1983), planning was underway for the largest spin-off in history. This spin-off will result from an agreement between the Justice Department and American Telephone and Telegraph Company to settle an antitrust suit filed by the Justice Department in 1974. The agreement, which was reached in January 1982 and approved in August 1982, will take effect on January 1, 1984.

At the time of the agreement, American Telephone owned 22 operating companies, Western Electric Co., which manufactured communications equipment, and Bell Laboratories, Inc., a premier research institution. Under the terms of the settlement, the 22 operating companies will be reorganized into seven regional holding companies which will be spun off on January 1, 1984. Cost of the breakup has been estimated to be at least $1.9 billion.

The regional operating companies will manage local telephone service, provide some intrastate long distance service on an exclusive basis, and publish directories (including the very profitable Yellow Pages). They may also provide cellular mobile phone service, market telephones (beginning in 1984), and offer other services. American Telephone will retain Western Electric, Bell Laboratories, and its newly established marketing arm, American Bell.

The settlement was reached as the trial of the federal antitrust case was nearing its end, and it seemed likely that American Telephone would lose. In denying a motion to dismiss the case, Judge Greene said, "the testimony and documentary evidence adduced by the government demonstrate that the Bell System has violated the antitrust laws in a number of ways over a lengthy period. . . ." By reaching a settlement, American Telephone avoided the possible forced divestiture of Western Electric and parts of Bell Laboratories which the Justice Department had been seeking. In addition, the settlement forestalled efforts pending in Congress to restructure American Telephone legislatively and to increase regulation of the communications industry.

Shareholders who own American Telephone stock in December 1983 (on the record date) will receive one share in each of the seven regional companies for each ten shares of American Telephone owned. Since American Telephone had about 3.2 million stockholders, it was expected that more than 22 million shareholder accounts would exist following the spin-off. Details of the transfer of ownership are provided in Figure 1.1.

To handle the massive amounts of paper work involved in the distribution of the new shares, American Telephone established a service center near Jacksonville, Florida, employing several thousand people. It was anticipated that the new center would continue to provide services to American Telephone and the seven operating companies following the spin-off. The center would provide a single location to handle record keeping, security transfers and inquiries and to administer dividend reinvestment and stock purchase plans. Also, the center would handle dividend payments and mailings to security holders.

The remainder of this book is devoted to a detailed examination of various aspects of corporate spin-offs. Chapter 2 describes and illustrates with multiple examples seven motives which corporate executives have given for undertaking spin-offs. Chapter 3 covers various mechanical aspects of spin-offs such as the plan of reorganization, the proxy statement, and the prospectus. Asset transfers, arrangements in connection with stock options and pension plans, and the hiring of experts also are discussed. Chapter 4 discusses the accounting and tax aspects of spin-offs, and Chapter 5 examines whether spin-offs have resulted in increases in shareholder wealth.

Chapters 6, 7, 8, and 9 provide case studies of individual spin-offs. Each was selected to highlight a different aspect of the topic. Chapter 6 examines the family of spin-offs undertaken by Tandy Corporation. One of the com-

Figure 1.1

Fourth Quarter 1982

SHARE OWNERS NEWSLETTER

Letter from the Chairman of the Board

December 16, 1982

Dear Share Owner:

We have filed with the Court a reorganization plan detailing the steps we propose to take in implementing the Consent Decree announced last January and approved in August.

As you know, the Consent Decree requires AT&T to divest the local portions of the Bell System's 22 operating companies.

The reorganization plan is the culmination of 11 months of arduous planning and preparation by the officers and managers of AT&T, the companies to be divested and other Bell System units. It represents our best effort not only to comply with the letter and spirit of the agreement but to provide a foundation upon which all parts of this enterprise can build for the future.

No aspect of the reorganization has received more careful attention than those matters directly affecting our share owners.

We sought, successfully I believe, to develop arrangements that would be equitable to all 3.2 million AT&T share owners and that would minimize any burden that divestiture might cause. In particular, we kept in mind throughout these months those share owners with smaller accounts who are less accustomed to stock transactions than investors with larger accounts.

Until now we have not been in a position to provide details of our planning, and I am glad that now we can. Most of this Newsletter is devoted to a discussion of the arrangements we have proposed, although they must still await final confirmation by the Court.

As we reported to you previously, we plan to group the 22 operating companies into seven regional holding companies, and–on January 1, 1984–to spin off ownership of the seven companies to AT&T share owners. For share owners, the key elements of that transfer of ownership are as follows:

1. The number of shares of AT&T common stock that you hold will not change, and new certificates will not be issued for these shares. If, for example, you own 50 shares of AT&T stock before divestiture, you will own 50 shares of AT&T stock after divestiture. If you own five shares before, you will own five afterward. After divestiture, of course, AT&T shares will represent ownership in a smaller company, and their market value will change accordingly.

2. Shares of the regional companies will be spun off at a 1:10 ratio. Thus, for each 10 shares of AT&T common stock you hold, you will acquire one share of common voting stock in *each* of the seven regional companies. So if you own, say, 50 shares of AT&T stock at the time of divestiture, you would then own five shares in each of the regional companies in addition to your AT&T stock. Accordingly, after divestiture your investment would be represented by a total of 85 shares of stock: 50 shares of AT&T and five shares in each of the seven regional companies.

3. However, share owners holding fewer than 10 shares of AT&T common stock–and thus not entitled to a full share in each regional company–will, after divestiture, be sent cash in lieu of fractional shares. (Such share owners will, of course, continue to hold their AT&T shares.) About 17 percent of our 3.2 million share owners are in this category, although their holdings rep-

Figure 1.1 *(continued)*

resent only about one-quarter of one percent of the total shares outstanding. To receive shares in the regional companies rather than cash, these share owners can purchase additional stock in 1983. To buy stock with no commission charge, share owners can enroll some or all of their shares in the AT&T Dividend Reinvestment and Stock Purchase Plan–if they have not already done so–and then send payment to AT&T for additional shares.

4. Share owners holding 500 or more shares of AT&T common stock will be sent certificates for their whole shares of regional company stock, probably in February 1984. They will receive cash in lieu of any fractional shares in the regional companies. In addition, they will have the opportunity to enroll in Dividend Reinvestment and Stock Purchase Plans to be established by the regional companies. Such share owners, comprising six percent of AT&T's stockholder accounts, hold approximately 70 percent of the outstanding stock.

5. Share owners holding at least 10 but fewer than 500 shares of AT&T common stock will be offered three choices in arranging their holdings in the regional companies. Such share owners hold approximately 30 percent of the outstanding AT&T stock, and account for 77 percent of the company's stockholders. These options, which are responsive to requests received from many share owners with accounts of this size, are as follows:

A. Share owners may receive certificates for their whole shares in one or more of the regional companies and cash in lieu of any fractional shares.

B. For each regional company, share owners may deposit all their shares–including fractional shares–in that regional company's Dividend Reinvestment and Stock Purchase Plan.

C. Share owners may ask that their stock in one or more of the regional companies be sold and the proceeds invested in one or more of the other regional companies. Orders would be accumulated so that lower brokerage fees could be obtained. Share owners would pay an appropriate fee for these transactions. Under this Option C, share owners can determine for each regional company whether to receive stock certificates (and cash for fractional shares) or to deposit their full and fractional shares in regional company dividend reinvestment accounts.

In January 1984, share owners holding at least 10 but fewer than 500 AT&T shares will receive a return mail card on which to give AT&T instructions for the handling of their regional company shares according to the choices listed above.

Information about AT&T and the prospective regional companies will be provided to assist share owners in making post-divestiture investment decisions.

By offering these options to share owners wishing to consolidate their regional company shares, we expect to reduce the costs they would otherwise incur in trading a small number of shares. In addition, the preparation and distribution of stock certificates in small amounts to so many share owners would be costly and difficult to complete in a reasonable period of time following divestiture. Nonetheless, share owners with smaller accounts will, if they so request, receive all their certificates in the seven regional companies at the same time the larger accounts are issued their certificates.

Some share owners have asked whether we plan to make arrangements to enable them to convert their regional company holdings into

Some questions and answers

How much will I receive for fractional shares of my regional company stock? That cannot yet be determined. It will depend on the prices at which regional company stocks are traded.

Is there any tax liability associated with the distribution of regional company stock? From a tax standpoint, share owners should not recognize a gain or loss when they receive their distribution of regional company shares. Sales of a regional company's shares and receipt of cash in lieu of a regional company's shares, however, are taxable transactions. When information about the regional companies is mailed to share owners before divestiture, tax information will be included.

How much will fees be for share owners with small accounts who arrange to have their regional company holdings consolidated? A fee schedule has not yet been determined. However, it is expected that for most eligible share owners the fees charged will be lower than fees obtainable if they were to make the same transactions on their own.

Figure 1.1 *(continued)*

AT&T stock. We do not. Our aim is to make it relatively easy for smaller share owners to consolidate their regional company stock, not to facilitate the shifting of stock away from the regional companies to AT&T. After all, most of the investment underlying the present AT&T stock is in assets which will go with the regional companies so that, at the time of distribution, each shareholder will hold stocks in several companies owning the same assets that are now represented by AT&T stock.

In the coming months, we will take a number of preliminary steps to set the stage for divestiture. Assuming that by April we receive court approval for our divestiture plan, we would begin reorganization according to the following schedule:

- By September, the assets going to the regional companies would be substantially assigned so that separate financial statements can be prepared.
- In October or November, the regional companies' Boards of Directors would be formed.
- In October or November these boards would announce their companies' dividends for the first quarter of 1984. At about the same time, AT&T would announce its dividend for the same period. These steps would facilitate the trading of regional company and AT&T stock on a post-divestiture basis.
- Also in October or November, AT&T and the regional companies would file with the Securities and Exchange Commission the documents necessary for the distribution and trading of regional company stock. Included in the filing would be material which would be mailed subsequently to share owners.
- At about the same time, the regional companies would file applications to list their common stock on the New York Stock Exchange and on any regional stock exchange they may choose.

- In November or December 1983, trading of the regional company common stock on the New York Stock Exchange would begin on a "when-issued" basis and would continue in this manner until the initial distribution of stock certificates to share owners in February. A "when-issued" market will establish price levels for the regional companies' stocks, which in turn will help to give our share owners and other investors a basis for evaluating these companies. (When shares are traded "when issued," settlement is delayed until the sellers are able to deliver their stock certificates.)
- A record date in December 1983 would be established for divestiture. (Thus, under the arrangements described above, stock in the regional companies would be distributed to holders of AT&T stock as of the record date.)

What to expect

In summary, as a share owner you will see divestiture unfold as follows:

- Near the end of 1983 you will receive materials describing the regional companies.
- In January 1984, you will receive a statement of account listing the number of AT&T shares you hold and the number of regional company shares you are to receive. If you hold at least 10 but fewer than 500 AT&T shares, you will also be sent the return mail card enabling you to select among the options described earlier.
- In February 1984, the initial mailing of certificates for regional company stock will take place.

This, then, is how we plan to proceed in the coming year. And, as the year unfolds, we will continue to keep you informed.

C. L. Brown

C. L. Brown

Why don't you plan to offer share owners with 500 or more shares of stock the consolidation options you will give to those with fewer than 500 shares. Generally speaking, the savings in brokerage costs gained by those eligible for the consolidation option will be roughly comparable to the trading advantages already enjoyed by share owners trading larger blocks of shares.

Will holders of AT&T preferred stock receive shares in the regional companies? No. Regional company stock will be distributed only to holders of AT&T common stock.

How did you arrive at a distribution ratio of 1:10? We sought a ratio that would result in an appropriate trading price range for the regional company stock and that would be simple to understand and calculate.

Will the dividends the various companies will announce late in 1983 add up to the $1.35 quarterly dividend AT&T stock is now paying? It will be an important goal of the regional companies and AT&T to be consistent with share owner desires and with patterns expected by the financial markets. In addition, it is not expected that

Figure 1.1 *(continued)*

---

divestiture as such would impair the collective dividend-paying ability of the separate entities after divestiture. Economic conditions and, in particular, fair treatment by regulatory agencies will determine the earnings and, thus, the dividend-paying ability of each company after divestiture.

What kind of dividend reinvestment plans will the regional companies have? Although we anticipate that all regional companies will have dividend reinvestment plans, the companies

themselves will make that determination and announce the details at a later time.

How can I get answers to other questions I may have? We have attempted in this Newsletter to give a comprehensive outline of the information now available about the distribution of regional company stock. However, if you need a clarification, we have established a special number you may call from 9 a.m. to 4:30 p.m. Eastern time: 800 221-1284. For all other stock and bond matters, please continue as usual to call 800 631-3311 or, from New Jersey, 800 352-4900.

---

panies spun off by Tandy also has had subsequent spin-offs. All of these spin-offs were undertaken to improve managerial efficiency. The spin-off of Louisiana Pacific by Georgia-Pacific to settle an antitrust complaint (described in Chapter 7) illustrates an involuntary spin-off. Chapter 8 examines the spin-off of Pengo Industries from Gearhart-Owen Industries to resolve managerial differences concerning investment policies. Chapter 9 describes the reorganization and spin-off undertaken by Santa Anita Consolidated, Inc. to achieve major tax savings. Chapter 10 provides a summary of the book that highlights the major findings and conclusions.

NOTES

1. See Bettauer (1967), Hayes (1972), Levitt (1975), and Alberts and McTaggart (1979) for a discussion of divestitures.

2. See Alberts and Segall (1966), Hogarty (1970), Levy and Sarnat (1970), Lintner (1971), Weston and Mansinghka (1971), Halpern (1973), Melicher and Rush (1973), Mandelker (1974), Haugen and Langtieg (1975), Firth (1978), and Mueller (1979) for a discussion of mergers.

REFERENCES

W. W. Alberts and J. M. McTaggart, "The Divestiture Decision: An Introduction," *Mergers and Acquisitions* (Fall 1979): 18-30.

W. W. Alberts and J. E. Segall, eds., *The Corporate Merger*. Chicago: University of Chicago Press, 1966.

A. Bettauer, "Strategy for Divestment," *Harvard Business Review* (April 1967): 116-24.

M. Firth, "Synergism in Mergers: Some British Results," *Journal of Finance* (May 1978): 670-72.

P. J. Halpern, "Empirical Estimates of the Amount and Distribution of Gains to Companies in Mergers," *Journal of Business* (October 1973): 554-75.

R. A. Haugen and T. C. Langtieg, "An Empirical Test for Synergism in Merger," *Journal of Finance* (September 1975): 1003-14.

R. H. Hayes, "New Emphasis on Divestment Opportunities," *Harvard Business Review* (July-August 1972): 55-64.

T. F. Hogarty, "The Profitability of Corporate Mergers," *Journal of Business* (July 1970): 317-27.

B. Lev and G. Mandelker, "The Micro Economic Consequences of Corporate Mergers," *Journal of Business* (January 1972): 85-104.

T. Levitt, "Dinosaurs Among the Bears and Bulls," *Harvard Business Review* (January-February 1975): 44-53.

H. Levy and M. Sarnat, "Diversification, Portfolio Analysis and the Uneasy Case for Conglomerate Mergers," *Journal of Finance* (September 1970): 795-802.

J. Lintner, "Expectations, Mergers and Equilibrium in Purely Competitive Securities Markets," *American Economic Review* (1971): 101-111.

F. A. Lovejoy, *Divestment for Profit*. New York: Financial Executives Research Foundation, 1971.

G. Mandelker, "Risk and Return: The Case of Merging Firms," *Journal of Financial Economics* (December 1974): 303-55.

R. W. Melicher and D. R. Rush, "The Performance of Conglomerate Firms: Recent Risk and Return Experience," *Journal of Finance* (May 1973): 381-88.

D. C. Mueller, "A Theory of Conglomerate Mergers," *Quarterly Journal of Economics* (November 1979): 643-60.

F. Weston and S. K. Mansinghka, "Test of the Efficiency Performance of Conglomerate Firms," *Journal of Finance* (September 1971): 919.

2

Reasons for Spin-Offs

This chapter describes the primary reasons for corporate spin-offs. These may be categorized as follows: (1) managerial considerations, (2) capital market conditions, (3) risk effects, (4) tax benefits, (5) marketing considerations, (6) regulatory factors, and (7) legal factors. Each of these will be discussed in turn, and specific examples of spin-offs illustrating each reason will be given. Of course, any particular spin-off may be motivated by several reasons. Much of the information presented is based on a review of prospectuses, proxy statements, and annual reports of those companies that were involved in spin-offs.

MANAGERIAL CONSIDERATIONS

Many corporate spin-offs are believed to provide managerial benefits to the parent firm and spun-off firm. Usually, these firms operate in disparate lines of business with different business environments, each with its own unique managerial and operational problems. Prior to a spin-off, the spun-off firm, operating as a wholly-owned subsidiary, often does not receive the management attention, as well as capital and other necessary support, required to pursue its profit and growth objectives. Further, it is difficult to gauge employee and executive performance and provide incentives because of the divergent lines of business. By separating these businesses via a spin-off, management often thinks that each firm will fare better because of improved managerial decision-making and greater managerial incentives.

Because the parent firm and spun-off firm will each have a specialized management reporting to a separate board of directors, there will be a better framework for management decisions concerning the employment of capital and the operation of the separate businesses. Parent firms naturally place primary emphasis on their most important businesses. After the spin-off, the parent firm will be able to give maximum support to its remaining businesses without being concerned with the spun-off subsidiary. Because the operational and financial progress of the businesses will be more visible to stockholders, the separate businesses will provide a stimulus to executives to show growth and improvement. There will be a clearer basis for evaluations and a correspondingly more accurate appraisal of performance by employees, the public, and the investment community.

Tandy Corporation, a marketer of leisure and other products through a nationwide chain of retail stores, spun off two subsidiaries concurrently—Tandycrafts, Inc. and Tandy Brands, Inc. Subsequently, Tandycrafts spun off Stafford-Lowdon, Inc., a subsidiary engaged in a general printing business, and several years later, spun off Color Tile, Inc. The stated objectives of all of these spin-offs were (1) to allow a more intensive management leadership of each company, (2) to provide a better environment for management decisions concerning both investment opportunities and operations, (3) to stimulate executives to show growth by creating increased visibility, and (4) to permit a clearer basis for evaluation.

Olin Corporation, a diversified manufacturer of chemicals, metals, and other products, spun off its wholly-owned forest products subsidiary, Olinkraft, Inc. Olin's management stated that Olin and Olinkraft faced very different business environments that could be dealt with more effectively by specialized managements reporting to separate boards of directors. After the spin-off, Olin could fully support the growth programs of all of its remaining businesses, particularly its chemical business. With its own listed stock, Olinkraft would be able to consider growth opportunities that might not be available to it as a subsidiary of Olin.

The spin-off of Easco Corporation's steel-making business operated by its wholly-owned subsidiary, Eastmet Corporation, was believed to offer several advantages to Easco's shareholders. Easco's stainless steel manufacturing business required capital investment generally larger than the capital needs of Easco's other lines of business. While Easco continued to improve the facilities of the stainless steel making business, the competing demands of the other lines of business requiring less massive investment began to require the firm to make choices regarding its investment opportunities. Management believed that the separation of the steel-making operations from its other businesses would provide a better framework for decisions concerning capital expenditures to be made by both companies.

As Easco diversified into different lines of business, the relationship of employee and executive performance to corporate operating results necessarily became more indirect, making it more difficult to relate employee performance to appropriate incentives. Management concluded that the separation would result in an improved ability to provide employee and executive incentives tied directly to corporate earnings and provide a better basis for the evaluation of executive performance.

Managerial considerations were an important factor in the spin-off of Cole National Corporation's consumer products group operated by Cole Consumer Products, Inc., a wholly-owned subsidiary. Because of its much larger size, Cole's specialty retailing businesses received greater management attention than that given to the consumer products group. Accordingly, Cole's management concluded that the spin-off would provide distinctive and specialized management leadership for the two fundamentally different businesses. This would provide an improved setting for management decisions concerning the employment of capital and the operations of the separate businesses and would help the executives of the two firms to maintain management excellence.

Tyler Corporation spun off Cronus Industries, Inc. primarily because it was the smallest and least profitable of Tyler's operations. Tyler's stated objective was to have a few large subsidiaries, each making a significant contribution to net income. Cronus clearly would never have obtained that objective because of the limited size of the market for the company's products (Cronus designs and fabricates heat transfer equipment for the electrical power generating industry). In addition, expansion of Cronus would have required a major investment in fixed assets which Tyler did not believe would have yielded an adequate return.

Tyler believed that Cronus, as an independent entity, would be better able to make acquisitions of a size that would be of interest and value to it, but that would be too small to be of interest to Tyler. In addition, Cronus could make acquisitions that might not be legal for Tyler because of antitrust laws and other regulatory prohibitions.

CAPITAL MARKET FACTORS

In several spin-offs the parent firm's management felt that investors did not properly value all of the parent firm's lines of business. By spinning off those subsidiaries that were believed to be undervalued, management expected that a number of benefits would be realized. Each company would be able to attract capital on a basis consistent with its respective businesses. As a result, the ability of each company to raise capital would be directly related to the relevant capital markets affecting its respective businesses. The separation would permit a clearer basis for the identification and evaluation of the business of each company by the investment community which could be an advantage when additional financing is needed. By increasing market visibility for the spun-off firm's growing business, some new investors might be persuaded to buy the firm's stock, thereby raising its value. The parent firm's value might also increase after the spin-off since the under-valued subsidiary would no longer dampen investor interest in the firm.

An example of a capital market induced spin-off involves Koger Proper-ties, Inc. which historically consisted of two distinct businesses. These two businesses were development and construction and property ownership and management. The development and construction business traditionally had provided investors with relatively volatile, high-risk investment opportun-ities. As a result, earnings were quite sensitive to the availability and cost of capital for real estate development, and to the strength of the national and local economies. But the ownership and management of rental office prop-erties, while also involving risks to the investor, was not as sensitive to those factors because completed, leased properties have established rental income and generally are financed through long-term mortgage indebtedness hav-ing fixed equal monthly payments of principal and interest. Koger Proper-ties, Inc.'s management felt that the development aspect of the company was never fully reflected in the marketplace. Accordingly, management be-lieved that it was in the interest of stockholders for the firm's two business activities to be conducted by separate and independent companies.

Another example is the spin-off by Alaska Airlines, Inc. of its wholly-owned subsidiary, Alaska Northwest Properties, Inc. (ANP), which held assets primarily unrelated to the airline industry. This spin-off was made partly due to management's view that Alaska Airlines's stock was under-valued because the market price did not fully reflect the nonairline assets owned by the airline through ANP. By spinning off ANP, Alaska Airlines forced the stock market to assign ANP a more realistic value.

Dillingham Corporation is a diversified company with principal busi-nesses in the maritime, energy, real estate, and construction industries. The board of directors of Dillingham concluded that its commercial real estate assets in Hawaii had a fair market value substantially in excess of their value as reflected in the market price for the firm's common stock. As part of a plan of partial liquidation, these real estate assets were transferred to a part-nership whose sole purpose was the liquidation of the real estate. Transfer-able depository receipts representing limited partnership interests were then distributed to Dillingham stockholders on the basis of one "partnership unit" for each share of stock.

Many spin-offs also have been related to mergers. Because these firms are typically concentrating on the merger rather than the spin-off, reasons for these spin-offs contained in company reports are usually not as detailed as for other types of spin-offs. Moreover, since the parent company (or some-times the spun-off firm) is merged into another firm, follow-up on the suc-cess of these spin-offs is more difficult.

It may be useful to describe briefly several spin-offs related to mergers. Under the terms of an agreement with Union Carbide Corporation, Rorer-Amchem, Inc. spun off its subsidiary, Amchem Products, Inc. Following the spin-off, Amchem Products merged into Union Carbide. Under the terms of a merger agreement between United Technologies Corporation and Dynell Electronics Corporation, Dynell spun off its subsidiary, Solid Photography, Inc. The stated purpose of the spin-off was to allow Dynell stockholders to continue to benefit from the economic potential of Solid Photography's products. The merger and spin-off also allowed favorable financing, previously unavailable, to support the development and marketing of Solid Photography's products. As a term of the merger, United Technologies agreed to lend Solid Photography $2 million. Also, at the time of the spin-off, Solid Photography issued rights to Dynell shareholders to purchase an additional 1.7 million shares of Solid Photography at $2.00 each. Another example of a spin-off related to a merger occurred in connection with the merger of Logistics Industries Corporation into Lydall, Inc. Just prior to the merger, Logistics spun off its Checkpoint Systems, Inc. subsidiary.

RISK EFFECTS

In many spin-offs, the parent firm and spun-off firm operate in very different lines of business, each having separate and distinct operating, financial, and investment characteristics. As a result, the two firms often have different operating or business risks as reflected in the volatility of earnings. In most cases, the spun-off firm is more risky. In these circumstances, one of the reasons frequently cited for the spin-off is to insulate each of the businesses from risks associated with the other.

After spinning off the more risky firm, the parent firm's earnings are more predictable and stable, lowering its overall cost of capital and increasing its borrowing capacity. Each firm will be able to finance future expansion on terms that are more in line with their historical and projected growth rates. A potential disadvantage is the inability to consolidate federal and state income tax returns. Also, financing may be more difficult after the spin-off because each company will not be able to rely on the earnings, cash flows, and assets of the other. A possible effect might be to lower the bond rating for the more risky firm.

The spin-off of Coastland Corporation of Florida from American Agronomics Corporation is an example where business risk differences were a major factor. American Agronomics Corporation is engaged primarily in the business of ownership and management of citrus groves and in citrus processing. Coastland Corporation, on the other hand, is involved primarily in the development and sale of homes and home sites. The board of directors of both firms concluded that it would be in the best interests of stockholders if these essentially different businesses were separated to: (1) insulate each of the businesses from risks associated with the other, (2) allow each enterprise to compete separately in relevant capital markets, which should enhance the ability of each company to obtain financing, (3) permit investors to make independent decisions regarding participation in real estate development and citrus investments, and (4) assist in improving the operation and performance of each of the businesses.

Another example is the spin-off of International Shipholding Corporation from Trans Union Corporation. These companies are engaged in two business activities which are basically dissimilar in nature. Trans Union charters or leases ocean-going vessels to others. International Shipholding Corporation actually operates ocean-going vessels. Over the years, Trans Union's chartering operations generally have been profitable on a fairly steady basis. By contrast, the direct shipping activities of International Shipping have been subject to wide fluctuations in revenues and profitability because of the uncertainties inherent in the fluctuating demand for vessels and world freight rates. Because of these fluctuations, Trans Union's management believed that the ownership of International Shipholding had not been favorable for Trans Union and its stockholders. Thus, management concluded that it would be in the best interests of Trans Union and its stockholders to terminate Trans Union's involvement in the direct operation of vessels by spinning off International Shipholding Corporation.

TAX BENEFITS

Significant tax benefits can be obtained through spin-offs in at least three ways. If the company's principal asset is real estate, it may be able to qualify as a real estate investment trust (REIT). Unlike other corporations whose dividends are payable only after payment of corporate income taxes, corporations which qualify as REITs may deduct dividends paid to shareholders from income before calculating their taxes. The result is that there is more income available for distribution to shareholders. Second, a firm may transfer income-producing property to a trust and distribute interests in the trust to its stockholders, thereby avoiding payment of corporate income taxes on income from the property. Third, if a United States based company derives significant revenues from overseas, it may be advisable to incorporate its foreign operations outside the United States and then spin off the resulting firm. The revenues of the spun-off firm are not taxed at United States corporate tax rates, but rather at the tax rates that prevail in the country of incorporation, which may be substantially lower than United States tax rates if they exist at all.

An excellent example of the REIT approach to tax savings through a spin-off is Santa Anita Consolidated, Inc. Santa Anita Consolidated owned and operated Santa Anita Park, a thoroughbred racetrack, and owned and developed commercial real estate properties for investment or sale. Santa Anita Consolidated merged into Santa Anita Realty Enterprises, Inc., a newly-formed Delaware corporation, and then spun off Santa Anita Operating Company, also a newly-formed Delaware corporation.

Santa Anita Realty Enterprises, Inc. will operate as a real estate investment trust under provisions of the Internal Revenue Code of 1954 and will own the racetrack property at Santa Anita Park and a portfolio of commercial real estate. Santa Anita Operating Company will conduct thoroughbred horse racing at Santa Anita Park and develop commercial real estate properties. The effect of this reorganization is substantially to increase the income available for distribution to stockholders because the REIT is not subject to federal income tax on income that it distributes to its stockholders.

An interesting feature of this reorganization is that the common stock of Santa Anita Realty Enterprises, Inc. and Santa Anita Operating Company is transferable only in units, each unit consisting of one share of common stock of each company. The shares of paired common stock are evidenced by the stock certificates being printed "back to back." In other words, the stock certificate for the operating company common stock is printed on the reverse side of the certificate of Realty Enterprises common stock. The reason for the pairing is that the two companies will continue to have a close business relationship so that common ownership will minimize questions of corporate opportunity and conflict of interest.

An innovative spin-off resulting in tax benefits was the spin-off of Mesa Royalty Trust (Trust) by Mesa Petroleum Co. (Company). Just prior to the spin-off, Trust was formed by Company to own a 90 percent net overriding royalty interest in certain Company producing oil and gas leases in the United States. The units of beneficial interest in Trust were then distributed to Company's stockholders. The result was to provide shareholders with a substantial income stream unburdened by corporate income tax.

An illustration of the derivation of tax benefits by spinning off foreign operations is the example of The Coastal Corporation (formerly Coastal States Gas Corporation). The Coastal Corporation, a Delaware corporation engaged in the international shipping business, spun off Coastal International, Ltd., a newly-formed Bermuda corporation. Coastal International, Ltd. is a foreign corporation organized in a jurisdiction that has no corporate income taxes. As a company incorporated and headquartered outside the United States, all of the company's earnings will be free of United States corporate taxes to the extent that such earnings are not connected effectively with a United States-based business conducted by the company or received by the company from sources within the United States.

Furthermore, if dividends are paid by the company to United States stockholders, they would be taxable only upon receipt by such stockholders. Accordingly, such dividends would avoid the "double taxation" which would apply if the dividends are paid first to the United States parent corporation and then paid to the stockholders of such a corporation. Another benefit is exemption of Coastal International from a number of United States laws including the anti-boycott provisions of the Internal Revenue Code and the Export Administration Act. Among other things, these laws may restrict dealings with Arab countries boycotting Israel.

A major reason for the spin-off of Gotaas-Larsen Shipping Corporation from IU International was also to avoid double taxation. Gotaas-Larsen Shipping Corporation, being incorporated in Liberia, has all of its earnings free of all corporate income tax, although some subsidiaries operating in certain jurisdictions do incur taxation. The company's principal office is located in Bermuda. Shares of the firm are traded on the London Stock Exchange and in the United States on the NASDAQ system. IU management regarded the spin-off as "the most important event in recent years" and felt that the separate companies could function more effectively in marketing their services and in raising capital.

Another illustration is the spin-off by Sea Containers, Inc. of Sea Containers Atlantic, Ltd., a Bermuda corporation engaged in the business of leasing marine container equipment outside of the United States to ocean carriers and others. In addition to tax benefits, management believed that some customers preferred to deal with a company neither organized in the United States nor controlled by a United States corporation. Freedom from United States legal and regulatory restrictions was also cited as a benefit. Shares of Sea Containers, Inc. and Sea Containers Atlantic, Ltd. are paired and printed on certificates "back to back."

Further examples of spin-offs followed by pairing of stock include the spin-offs of The L. E. Myers Co. International, Ltd. by The L. E. Myers Co., and RMP International, Ltd. by Parsons Corp. L. E. Myers (domestic) constructs transmission lines for electric utilities. Myers International, a Bermuda company, conducts a similar business principally in Saudi Arabia. The Parsons Corporation, one of the world's largest international engineering/construction organizations, spun off its subsidiary, RMP International, Ltd., which offers services similar to the parent, but exclusively outside the United States.

MARKETING CONSIDERATIONS

At least two different types of marketing considerations have been responsible for spin-offs. Several firms have spun off subsidiaries which were not closely related to their primary businesses. These spin-offs were designed to allay fears by customers, suppliers, and others that these firms were not committed to, and might end ˉparticipation in, these particular industries. Another type of spin-off motivated by marketing considerations was designed to separate potentially incompatible product lines.

Over a period of six years, MGM Grand Hotels, Inc. evolved from a company engaged primarily in filmed entertainment to a company obtaining a majority of its operating income from hotel/gaming operations. During this period, the number of motion pictures produced each year was reduced, and direct motion picture distribution was abandoned. A belief developed among many individuals in the entertainment industry that MGM Grand would not continue as a motion picture production company. As a result, MGM Grand found it more difficult to attract desirable projects and artists. Therefore, to improve its competitive position in the entertainment business, MGM Grand's management decided to transfer its entertainment business to a newly-formed subsidiary, Metro-Goldwyn-Mayer Film Co. (MGM Film), and to spin off the shares of MGM Film to MGM Grand's stockholders.

The principal purpose for the spin-off of GEO International Corporation by Peabody International Corporation was "to segregate like products and services into two separate entities, thereby making each a more significant entity in its respective field." In recent years, Peabody evolved from a company engaged primarily in the environmental control business to one obtaining much of its operating income by providing products and services to firms engaged in the production of oil and gas and from the testing and inspection of products for large industrial products (oil field/quality assurance businesses). Consequently, the company's management believed that there was confusion in the investment and business community as to the future direction of the company. This confusion imposed limitations on recruiting, marketing, asset management, financing, acquisitions, and perceptions of the company as an investment.

Separation of the environmental and oil field/quality assurance groups into two separate entities would, in management's view, greatly enhance the opportunities of each group in its own business. Because oil field/quality assurance companies commanded higher price/earnings ratios than environmental companies at the time of the spin-off, GEO's ability to raise equity capital from the public would be enhanced. Such a separation should also overcome the perception in the oil field/quality assurance communities that the company was essentially an environmental company that also engaged in these two businesses. This perception, in the past, had resulted in Peabody's oil field/quality assurance businesses not receiving the same opportunities to acquire projects and businesses as other companies whose primary activity was the oil field/quality assurance business. Peabody's management felt that there could be a rekindling of entrepreneurial spirit and initiative as the separate managements would feel that their individual efforts would make a significant difference on bottom line results.

Standex International Corporation manufactures a variety of consumer and industrial products. One subsidiary published religious materials while another, Bingo King Company, manufactured and sold a complete line of bingo items. Standex's management believed that "its religious publishing activities would be adversely affected should its continuing participation . . . in what is perceived as gambling activities, became widely known.'' Accordingly, Standex spun off Bingo King. Another benefit of the spin-off was that it freed Standex from regulations governing the gambling industry.

Calny, Inc. operated a number of restaurants including forty-six restaurant franchises obtained from Taco Bell. In 1972, when Taco Bell deemphasized its franchise program, Calny negotiated an agreement with Taco Bell allowing Calny to operate competing restaurants under the name "Taco Charley," provided these restaurants were not located within one mile of a Taco Bell restaurant. Subsequently, forty-three Taco Charley restaurants were opened. Recently, Taco Bell has again begun to emphasize its franchise program, but, because of Calny's ownership of Taco Charley, Taco Bell has been unwilling to grant Calny additional franchises. Moreover, Calny faced the prospect of not being able to renew its existing Taco Bell franchises. To overcome these difficulties, Calny spun off the Taco Charley subsidiary.

REGULATORY FACTORS

Regulatory factors have been the cause of both involuntary and voluntary spin-offs. Involuntary spin-offs are usually the result of a complaint filed by a federal or state regulatory agency. On the other hand, voluntary spin-offs are sometimes made to separate regulated and unregulated businesses.

CBS Inc. spun off Viacom International, Inc. to comply with rules of the Federal Communications Commission (FCC), which prevented television networks from engaging in domestic cable television (CATV) operations and also severely restricted their ability to do business in the worldwide film syndication field.

Another involuntary spin-off was the spin-off of Facet Enterprises, Inc. by the Bendix Corporation. Facet is engaged primarily in the manufacture and sale of filters and automotive components. The Federal Trade Commission (FTC) ordered the disposal of this business because of perceived violations of the antitrust laws. The FTC also forced the spin-off of Louisiana Pacific Corporation from Georgia-Pacific Corporation (GP) because it ruled that certain GP acquisitions could substantially lessen competition or tend to create a monopoly in the softwood plywood industry.

An involuntary spin-off precipitated by a state regulatory agency was the spin-off of Valero Energy Corporation by Coastal States Gas Corporation. Valero operated an interstate gas pipeline system in Texas. The company experienced an inability to purchase natural gas at prices below the price at which it was required to sell to many of its customers under long-term contracts. As a result, the company found it necessary to purchase gas at substantially higher prices than those historically existing in its market area for delivery to its customers under long-term gas sale contracts which did not contain provisions for passing on the increased costs. Unsuccessful efforts to renegotiate these contracts with its customers led the company to request that the Railroad Commission of Texas (which had regulatory jurisdiction) order rate relief. After several years of regulatory proceedings and litigation, a settlement plan was developed that included the spin-off of Valero Energy Corporation.

Three examples of regulation-induced voluntary spin-offs were the spin-off of Central Louisiana Electric Company, Inc. (CLECO) from Central Louisiana Energy Corporation, the spin-off of Primark Corporation from American Natural Resources Company, and the spin-off of Gibraltar Savings Association from Imperial Corporation of America. The purpose of the spin-off of CLECO by Central Louisiana Energy Corporation was to separate regulated and non-regulated activities. CLECO, an electric utility, is regulated by the Louisiana Public Service Commission with respect to rates and issuance of securities. No other part of Central Louisiana Energy Corporation's business was subject to similar regulation. Management felt that the affiliation of regulated and non-regulated businesses had caused problems.

The significant capital expenditures required by CLECO, particularly for generating facilities, coupled with the regulatory environment in which it operates, reduce flexibility and require long-term capital expenditures and financial planning. Central Louisiana Energy Corporation's non-utility subsidiaries involved in oil and gas related activities operate in a generally unregulated business environment and require different planning strategies. Lower risk and returns on investment are inherent in a regulated industry such as CLECO's when compared to the company's non-utility subsidiaries. Accordingly, management concluded that the separation of the electric utility business of CLECO and the oil and gas related businesses of Central Louisiana Energy Corporation's other subsidiaries would provide the necessary financial, operational, managerial, and regulatory flexibility for these dissimilar activities to achieve greater efficiency and growth.

Primark Corporation, a wholly-owned subsidiary of American Natural Resources Company (ANRC), is the largest natural gas distribution company in Michigan and is subject to the jurisdiction of the Michigan Public Service Commission (MPSC) as to rates, issuance of securities, and other matters. Because of its ownership of Primark, ANRC is subject to the Public Holding Company Act of 1935 which places restrictions on ANRC's ability to diversify its operations.

Primarily because of a decline in gas sales and inadequate and delayed rate relief from the MPSC, Primark's earnings in recent years failed to reach the earnings objectives of ANRC. ANRC believed that the failure of MPSC to provide adequate and timely rate relief for Primark was related, in part, to Primark's being part of ANRC. The need for fair rate treatment apparently was obscured by the overall operating result of ANRC. Separation of Primark from ANRC was expected to cause its rates and earnings to be evaluated by the MPSC more realistically.

Imperial Corporation of America is one of the largest multi-state savings and loan holding companies. One of the subsidiaries of Imperial was Gibraltar Savings Association of Houston, Texas. While Gibraltar could expand internally, Federal Home Loan Bank Board regulations prohibited Gibraltar from acquiring other savings associations because it was part of a multi-state savings and loan holding company. Hence, to eliminate this obstacle to Gibraltar's growth, Imperial spun off Gibraltar to Imperial's stockholders.

LEGAL FACTORS

Like the regulatory factors discussed above, legal factors have also resulted in both involuntary and voluntary spin-offs. A number of involuntary spin-offs resulted from the Bank Holding Company Act of 1969, which required companies whose business was not principally banking to divest themselves of ownership or control of commercial banks. Voluntary spin-offs are sometimes made by firms as a means of overcoming legal obstacles which prevent the firm from accomplishing its objectives.

Sperry and Hutchinson (S & H), whose principal business is (S & H Green) trading stamps, organized State National Bancorp, Inc. to acquire its 99.3 percent interest in State National Bank of Connecticut. All of Bancorp's shares were then distributed to S & H's stockholders. Similarly, American Financial Corporation spun off The Provident Bank.

The spin-off of Hotel Investors Corp. (HIC) by Hotel Investors Trust (HIT) illustrates a voluntary spin-off motivated by legal restrictions. HIT was organized as a REIT to invest primarily in hotel properties. To the extent that earnings are distributed to stockholders, a REIT does not pay federal income tax. But REITs are prohibited from actively managing property. To circumvent this prohibition, HIT organized HIC and spun off the shares of HIC to its (i.e., HIT's) shareholders. Each share of HIC is paired with a share of HIT so that both companies are owned by the same stockholders and stock certificates are printed "back to back." The pairing also allowed the shares of HIC to be traded immediately on the New York Stock Exchange in combination with those of HIT. Following the spin-off, HIC began to manage several of HIT's hotels, an activity that would have been prohibited for HIT prior to the spin-off. Also, note that the end result of this reorganization was a paired REIT and operating company similar to that for Santa Anita Companies discussed above under "Tax Benefits."

Mechanics of Corporate Spin-Offs

3

This chapter presents an overview of the process by which a spin-off is actually implemented. The chapter is not intended to be a comprehensive guide, but rather to provide information on many of the most important technical aspects of spin-offs. Perhaps this information will be useful to firms contemplating a spin-off.

Probably the most important mechanical aspect of the spin-off discussed in this chapter is the plan of reorganization which describes the details of the agreements between the parent and spun-off firm. Other aspects of the spin-off that are covered in this chapter include the registration statement and proxy statement for the spin-off (along with a discussion of how to obtain copies of these documents), use of various types of experts and adjustments for warrants, convertible securities, stock option plans, and pension plans. But first, a typical calendar of events for a spin-off is provided.

TYPICAL SPIN-OFF CALENDAR

Once the decision to spin off a subsidiary has been made, management should formulate a work plan. This work plan indicates, in detail, what steps must be taken to complete the spin-off, target dates for the completion of each step, and who is responsible for seeing that each step is completed on schedule.

To convey an idea of the timing of some of the major events leading up to a spin-off, significant dates for the spin-off of Santa Anita Operating Company by Santa Anita Realty Enterprises are presented below:

April 1979	Public announcement of plans for reorganization and spin-off
August 1979	Board of directors approves plan of reorganization
October 1979	Company receives favorable ruling from IRS
December 1979	Stockholders approve plan of reorganization
January 1980	Spin-off completed

These dates, taken primarily from Santa Anita's 1980 annual report, show that once management decides to spin off a subsidiary, necessary arrangements to complete the transaction can proceed quickly.

THE PLAN OF REORGANIZATION

The plan of reorganization is the agreement between the parent and subsidiary governing the details of the spin-off. The plan must be approved by the board of directors of both the parent and subsidiary, as well as by the stockholders of the parent. A complete description of the plan including the text of the actual agreement itself is often provided in the proxy statement which is sent to stockholders of the parent along with the announcement of the stockholders meeting at which the plan is to be voted upon; occasionally, the text of the plan is provided in the prospectus. Both the proxy statement and prospectus are discussed more fully below.

The plan of reorganization contains details of the mechanics of the spin-off, including the relationship between the parent and subsidiary during the period leading up to and following the spin-off. Any exchanges of assets and liabilities contemplated prior to the spin-off are indicated. If the subsidiary is to be spun off intact and in a form in which it has been operating for some time, less detail is provided in the plan concerning asset exchanges. On the other hand, if considerable restructuring of the assets and liabilities of the parent and subsidiary are to take place prior to the spin-off, more detail is required. For example, Koger Properties, Inc. transferred 136 office buildings to its subsidiary, The Koger Company, just prior to the spin-off of the subsidiary. The address of each property was listed in the plan of reorganization.

In addition to asset/liability exchanges, a variety of items typically are covered in the plan of reorganization. The number of shares of stock to be distributed, record and payment dates for the distribution, contemplated exchange listings, and other items related to the stock to be issued may be included. Items upon which the completion of the plan is conditioned are discussed; these may include stockholder and regulatory approvals, receipt of favorable tax rulings, and satisfactory legal opinions.

Preparation for the spin-off includes arrangements associated with the transfer of employees and revision of stock options, employee stock ownership plans, and pension plans. Each of these may require careful planning so as to assure fairness and equity to the parent and subsidiary and their respective employees.

There are few guidelines or strict limitations concerning the transfer of assets in the reorganization. Typically, assets and liabilities, as well as employees, directly associated with the subsidiary are spun off while direct obligations of the parent are unaffected. The proxy statement and prospectus contain actual and pro forma balance sheets and income statements for the parent and subsidiary which indicate how the assets and liabilities are to be divided. Following the spin-off, at least initially, the parent may continue to provide some administrative services (tax, legal, etc.), office space, and other assistance to the former subsidiary. For example, following its spin-off by Tandy Corporation, Tandy Brands continued to maintain its executive headquarters at Tandy Corporation's principal office. In addition, Tandy Corporation prepared certain tax returns and other reports and made fleet vehicle arrangements for Tandy Brands. Tandy Brands paid Tandy Corporation a fee based on the actual cost of the services provided plus 10 percent.

While there are few specific limitations on the transfer of assets in the reorganization, the parent may not be entirely free to do whatever the parent wants. This is best illustrated by the spin-off of Facet Enterprises, Inc. from The Bendix Corporation. As part of the reorganization plan leading to the spin-off, Facet assumed $70 million of unfunded pension liabilities, but only $18 million in assets. Following the spin-off, Facet complained to the Internal Revenue Service, which subsequently ordered Bendix to pay another $14.7 million to Facet's pension fund. Then, Facet sued Bendix charging that Bendix failed to fulfill its fiduciary duties toward Facet at the time when Facet was a wholly-owned subsidiary of Bendix. Ultimately, Facet accepted an out-of-court settlement in which Bendix agreed to drop its appeal of the Internal Revenue Service ruling and also to pay Facet another $4.3 million.

THE PROXY STATEMENT

As mentioned above, a proxy statement accompanies the notice of the meeting of the stockholders which is called to approve the plan of reorganization. While it is not feasible to reproduce the entire proxy statement and related documents here, Appendix A provides the following documents for Easco Corporation: (1) the letter to the stockholders, (2) the notice of the special stockholders' meeting, (3) the table of contents for the proxy statement, and (4) the introduction and summary for the proxy statement. Shareholders may also be asked to vote on amendments to the corporate charter and by-laws (perhaps to increase the number of shares outstanding or to approve various other technical matters) at the same stockholders' meeting.

THE REGISTRATION STATEMENT

The shares distributed in the spin-off must typically be registered with the Securities and Exchange Commission. The prospectus is the part of the registration statement which must be provided to stockholders who receive stock in the spin-off. Most of the items contained in the proxy statement are also covered in the registration statement. In fact, some firms have combined the proxy statement and prospectus into a single document (for an example see the proxy statement/prospectus for IU International Corporation). As with the proxy statement, it is not feasible to reproduce an entire registration statement, but Appendix B provides examples of the cover page, table of contents, and summary for the prospectus of Facet Enterprises, Inc.

OBTAINING DOCUMENTS FROM THE SECURITIES AND EXCHANGE COMMISSION

Managers contemplating spin-offs for their firms may be interested in obtaining copies of proxy statements, registration statements, prospectuses, or annual reports for firms which already have had spin-offs. These documents are public records available from the Securities and Exchange Commission. Perhaps the most convenient way to obtain this information is from Disclosure, Incorporated, 5161 River Road, Bethesda, Maryland, 20816 (telephone numbers—in Maryland: 301-951-1350; toll free number outside Maryland: 800-638-8241). Disclosure also has offices in New York City (732-5955) and Los Angeles (478-4441).

Disclosure provides several types of service. Current filings, as well as prior filings back to 1968, are available on paper or microfiche. Same-day, first-class mail service for paper copies costs $0.35 per page ($10.00 minimum per order) or $10.00 per filing (report) on microfiche. Delivery charges are extra. Air courier, messenger, and "on line" services are also available.

By writing the Securities and Exchange Commission directly, a cheaper but less speedy type of service is available. The charge is $0.10 per page plus shipping cost, with a minimum charge of $5.00. Service is usually provided within two weeks, but sometimes delays of as much as two additional weeks are experienced. Disclosure, Inc. is the contractor for this service.

WARRANTS, CONVERTIBLE SECURITIES, STOCK OPTIONS, AND RETIREMENT PLANS

The treatment of warrants and convertible securities depends on the terms of these securities as described in the corporate charter. Typically, the number of shares which can be obtained upon exercise or conversion is multiplied by the ratio of the market price of the parent firm's shares including and then excluding the value of the shares spun off. Both IU International and Easco Corporation adjusted the terms of their convertible preferred stock and convertible bonds in this way. At the time of the spin-off of Leasco Corporation, Reliance Group, Incorporated had both warrants and convertible debentures outstanding. No adjustments in the conversion or exercise prices of those securities were made as a result of the spin-off.

Many firms have established stock option plans for key employees. For those option-holders who remain employees of the parent after the spin-off, the terms of the options are generally adjusted (by increasing the number of shares which may be purchased under the option) so that the aggregate market value of the shares which may be purchased under the options is unchanged. A new exercise price is then calculated by dividing the total exercise price by the increased number of shares which may be purchased under the options.

Executives who become employees of the spun-off firm generally have their options in the parent firm replaced by options in the new firm. This is done in a way which maintains the aggregate market value of the shares purchasable under these options and also maintains the ratio of aggregate market value of shares purchasable to aggregate exercise value.

An example may be useful. Suppose an executive has an option to purchase 5,000 shares of the parent firm's stock at $10 per share (for an aggregate exercise price of $5,000 \times \$10 = \$50,000$). The market value of the stock is $20 per share prior to the spin-off ($5,000 \times \$20 = \$100,000$ aggregate market value) and $10 per share after the spin-off. Typically, following the spin-off these options would be adjusted to cover 10,000 shares with an exercise price of $5 per share. This preserves the aggregate exercise price of $50,000 ($10,000 \times \$5$) and the aggregate market value of shares which may be purchased, $100,000 ($10,000 \times \$10$).

Deferred compensation plans are usually adjusted in a manner similar to that of stock option plans just described.

A number of firms operate various types of employee stock purchase plans. Accounts in these plans which have been established for employees who become employees of the spun-off firm are generally transferred to similar plans established by the spun-off firm.

Most firms have established retirement plans for the benefit of their employees. Assets in the parent's plan attributable to employees of the subsidiary are typically transferred to a new plan established by the subsidiary. The subsidiary then assumes responsibility for the unfunded liability of its plan, including liabilities for prior service of all workers transferred to the subsidiary by the parent. In determining eligibility for and the amount of retirement benefits, years of service with the parent usually count as years of service with the subsidiary.

LEGAL, ACCOUNTING, AND OTHER EXPERTS

During the time preceding a spin-off, parent firms may employ a variety of experts. Public accountants examine the financial records of the parent and subsidiary. Legal counsel prepares the plan of reorganization, registration statement, applications for IRS rulings and other documents, reviews the tax consequences of the spin-off, attests to the fact that the shares issued are validly issued, fully-paid and nonassessable, and performs a variety of other tasks. A favorable tax ruling by the Internal Revenue Service is critical in completing many spin-offs.

Legal counsel may also help in obtaining the approval of any regulatory bodies which may be required. In the case of the spin-off of Color Tile by Tandycrafts, it was necessary to request that the Federal Reserve Board add Color Tile to its list of marginable over-the-counter stocks. Since the Color Tile shares to be spun off represented about 83 percent of the value of Tandycrafts (which was listed on the New York Stock Exchange), the price of Tandycrafts could be expected to fall about 83 percent following the spin-off. (A precise estimate of the value of Color Tile stock was available since 1 million Color Tile shares had been sold to the public several months prior to the spin-off.) If the Federal Reserve Board had not granted the request to add Color Tile shares to the list of marginable over-the-counter stocks, stockholders of Tandycrafts who held their stock in margin accounts could have received substantial margin calls.

Other experts in addition to lawyers and accountants may also be employed. In conjunction with its spin-off of Gotaas-Larsen Shipping Corporation, IU International Corporation employed Merrill Lynch White Weld to investigate the fairness to IU stockholders of the proposed spin-off. Since Gotaas-Larsen was a foreign corporation, Hambros Bank Limited, London, was also engaged to investigate and attest to the fairness of the spin-off. Letters from both Merrill Lynch White Weld and Hambros Bank Limited appear in the prospectus describing the spin-off.

The spin-off of Santa Anita Operating Company by Santa Anita Realty Enterprises was a taxable distribution resulting in ordinary income to stockholders. Paine, Webber, Jackson and Curtis, Incorporated was employed to determine the fair market value of Operating Company at the time of the reorganization. Easco Corporation retained Reynolds Securities, Inc. to review its spin-off of Eastmet. In addition to an assessment as to the fairness of the proposed spin-off, the opinion of Reynolds covered topics not typically included in similar opinions prepared in connection with other spin-offs. Reynolds also stated its belief that the proposed division of assets and liabilities would allow both firms to be financially viable and that the reorganization would facilitate evaluation of the two firms by investment analysts.

4

Accounting and Tax Aspects of Spin-Offs

This chapter is not intended to provide a comprehensive guide to the accounting and tax aspects of spin-offs, but rather is intended to introduce the reader to many of the issues involved. Because of the complexity of these issues, expert advice is obviously necessary in connection with each spin-off.

The accounting and tax treatments of spin-offs are explained in this chapter. The proper accounting treatment of spin-offs is described in Accounting Principles Board (APB) Opinion No. 29, which deals with nonmonetary transactions, and APB Opinion No. 30, which specifies the accounting and reporting for disposal of a segment of a business. It is obviously advantageous for the proceeds of a spin-off to be treated as a tax-free distribution. For a spin-off to be a tax-free distribution, it must conform to the requirements of Section 355 of the Internal Revenue Code of 1954.[1]

To illustrate the nature of spin-offs, designate shareholders as $I(1)$, $I(2)$, $I(3)$, . . . , $I(n)$, the parent or investor company as P and the subsidiary or investee company as S. Although 100 percent ownership is not a requirement for a distribution to be classified as a spin-off, hereafter assume 100 percent ownership in all cases. The situation prior to the spin-off is shown diagrammatically in Figure 4.1.

Now assume P makes a prorata distribution of all of S's stock to P's stockholders. This distribution is a spin-off, and Figure 4.2 illustrates the results.

The ownership interest of $I(1)$ through $I(n)$ in companies P and S remains unchanged after the spin-off, but the interest in S is owned directly instead of indirectly through ownership of P.

Figure 4.1

Ownership Prior to Spin-Off

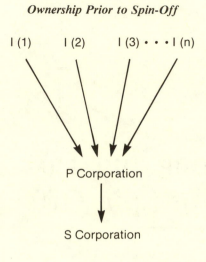

Source: Prepared by the author.

Figure 4.2

Ownership After Spin-Off

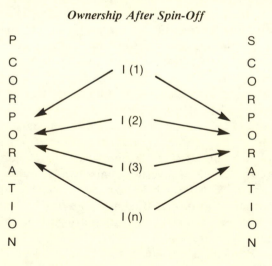

Source: Prepared by the author.

ACCOUNTING TREATMENT OF SPIN-OFFS

APB Opinion No. 29, "Accounting for Nonmonetary Transactions," applies to spin-offs because spin-offs involve nonreciprocal transfers of nonmonetary assets from an enterprise to its owners. Typically, there is a distribution of all or a significant part of the capital stock of one or more subsidiaries (nonmonetary assets) to stockholders. The transactions are nonreciprocal in that the transfers are in one direction (e.g., from an enterprise to its owners).

According to APB Opinion No. 29, accounting for the distribution of nonmonetary assets to owners of an enterprise in a spin-off or other form of reorganization or liquidation (or in a plan that is in substance the recession of a prior business combination) should be based on recorded amounts (after reduction, if applicable, for an indicated impairment of value) of the nonmonetary asset distributed. The Opinion considers a spin-off to be "a prorata distribution to owners of an enterprise of shares of a subsidiary or other investee company that has been or is being consolidated or that has been or is being accounted for under the equity method. . . ."[2] The APB holds that because the distribution was "prorata," the overall nature of the total business is the same after the spin-off as it was before. Accordingly, this event is recorded at book values and no gains are recognized. But losses are always recognized when sustained. A numerical example will illustrate these principles.

Assume that P spins off S by distributing all 50,000 shares of S's stock to P's shareholders. The book value per share of S's stock is $10. In accordance with APB Opinion No. 29, the proper accounting treatment for the spin-off of S by P is shown in Table 4.1.

Table 4.1
APB Opinion No. 29, Accounting Treatment of a Hypothetical Spin-Off*

P's investment in S at the date of the spin-off	Retained earnings Investment in S	$500,000 $500,000
Assume P spins off S when the fair value of S stock is above book value	Retained earnings Investment in S	$500,000 $500,000
Assume P spins off S when the fair value of S stock is $8 per share**	Loss on spin-off of S Retained earnings Investment in S	$100,000 $400,000 $500,000

*All indented entries are credits. All other entries are debits.

**Assume that the fair value of S stock is an indication of the fair value of S's net assets.

Notice in Table 4.1 that if S is spun off at a price above book value no gain is realized and the transaction is based on recorded amounts. But when S has a fair market value less than the book value, losses are recognized. Specifically, with a book value of $10 per share and fair value of $8 per share, a loss of $2 per share is sustained, which totals $100,000 for 50,000 shares.

APB Opinion No. 30 describes the accounting and reporting for disposal of a segment of a business such as through a spin-off. The Opinion states that the term "segment of a business" refers to a component of an entity whose activities represent a separate major line of business or class of customers that can be clearly distinguished physically, operationally, and for financial reporting purposes from the other assets, operations, and activities of the entity. Many spin-offs possess this characteristic. If the assets being disposed of are not clearly separable from other assets of the entity, it is strongly suggested that the transaction should not be classified as the disposal of a segment of the business.

According to Opinion No. 30, operations of a segment that has been or will be discontinued should be reported separately as a component of income before extraordinary items and the cumulative effect of accounting changes (if applicable). The Opinion further states, "amounts of income taxes applicable to the results of discontinued operations and the gain or loss from disposal of the segment should be classified on the face of the income statement or in related notes. Revenues applicable to the discontinued operations should be separately disclosed in the related notes." With regard to earnings per share data, the Opinion recommends that per share data for the results of discontinued operations and gain or loss from disposal of the business segment may be included on the face of the income statement or in a related note.

An example of the accounting treatment of spin-offs is provided by the records of the spin-off by Oxford Industries, Inc. of its wholly-owned subsidiary, Lanier Business Products, Inc., which was effected under a plan of reorganization. Lanier is engaged primarily in the manufacture, sale, and service of dictation equipment and the distribution and service of visual display text editing typewriters and other business equipment. Oxford is engaged in the design, manufacture, and sale of consumer apparel products.

The spin-off of Lanier was recorded on the books as of June 3, 1977. Consistent with APB Opinion No. 30, the earnings of the spun-off operations are shown separately from Oxford's continuing operations in Table 4.2.

On a historical basis, the assets and liabilities of the Lanier operations had been owned through various subsidiaries and a division of Oxford. Through an internal reorganization on May 28, 1976, the business products operations were combined in a wholly-owned subsidiary, Lanier Business Products, Inc. But in connection with the reorganization, certain assets and

Table 4.2

Oxford Industries, Inc. and Subsidiaries Consolidated Summary of Earnings,
Year End, June 3, 1977*

Net Sales	$220,484,000
Cost and Expenses	209,261,000
Interest	1,507,000
Income Taxes	4,578,000
Earnings from Continuing Operations	5,138,000
Earnings from Spun-Off Operations (net of applicable income taxes)	6,725,000
Net Earnings	$ 11,863,000
Earnings per Common Share	
From Continuing Operations	$1.83
From Spun-Off Operations	2.40
Net Earnings per Share	$4.23

Source: Oxford Industries, Inc. 1977 10-k report.

*Notes that accompany this financial statement are not reproduced.

liabilities arising from Business Products's operations were retained by Oxford. Accordingly, these accounts are not included in the consolidated balance sheets of Lanier as of June 3, 1977, and May 28, 1976. A summary of the impact of the reorganization on the balance sheet of Lanier at May 28, 1976, is shown in Table 4.3.

As shown in Table 4.3, Oxford retained $13,459,000 of assets and assumed $17,034,000 of liabilities. The difference of $3,575,000 represented a contribution of capital to Lanier by Oxford. Subsequently, Lanier paid a dividend to Oxford of $5 million by cancelling indebtedness of Oxford in that amount.

Lanier continued to administer collection of the installment contracts retained by Oxford and continued to service the related equipment. Under an agreement dated May 20, 1977, Oxford became obligated to pay to Lanier the portion of the contract collections it receives that are attributable to finance charges and service contract income. Accordingly, the financial statements of Lanier for the year ending June 3, 1977, included the finance charges and service contract income arising from the installment contracts retained by Oxford.

In March 1977, Oxford made an additional contribution to the capital of

Table 4.3

Summary of the Impact of the Spin-Off on Lanier's Balance Sheet at May 28, 1976

ASSETS	Balances at May 28, 1976 Prior to Transfer	Items Retained by Oxford	Dividend Paid to Oxford	Balances at May 28, 1976 After Transfer
Cash...............................	$ 25,000	$ (20,000)	$	$ 5,000
Receivables:				
Regular trade	11,355,000	(11,355,000)		
Installment contracts	20,666,000	(3,613,000)		17,053,000
Less:				
Allowance for bad debts	500,000	(500,000)		
Unearned finance charges	6,238,000	(1,029,000)		5,209,000
	25,283,000	(13,439,000)		11,844,000
Inventories	11,086,000			11,086,000
Property, plant and equipment	1,010,000			1,010,000
Other assets........................	1,156,000			1,156,000
	38,560,000	(13,459,000)		25,101,000
LIABILITIES				
Accounts payable....................	2,083,000			2,083,000
Income taxes.......................	5,309,000	(3,080,000)		2,229,000
Unearned income on service contracts ...	6,489,000	(1,452,000)		5,037,000
Other current liabilities	4,769,000	(29,000)		4,740,000
Due to (from) Oxford Industries, Inc. ...	1,928,000	(12,473,000)	5,000,000	(5,545,000)
Long-term debt	244,000			244,000
	20,822,000	(17,034,000)	5,000,000	8,788,000
Net assets	$17,738,000	$(3,575,000)	$5,000,000	$16,313,000

Source: Lanier Business Products, Inc. 1977 Annual Report.

Lanier of $2,078,000 for the purpose of giving Lanier the benefit of the cumulative net earnings of the business products division of Oxford, which historically had been included in retained earnings of Oxford.

TAX TREATMENT OF SPIN-OFFS

The statutory and nonstatutory requirements that define the tax status of corporate spin-offs are complex and often unclear, and, as a result, have required considerable interpretation by the courts and the Internal Revenue Service (IRS). Accordingly, corporate executives who are contemplating a spin-off are advised to seek a private letter ruling before proceeding with the spin-off. This section reviews the various requirements for a tax-free spin-off. Section 355 of the Internal Revenue Code is the principal statute governing the tax aspects of corporate spin-offs.[3] According to Wellen (1980),[4] for a spin-off to be a tax-free distribution under Section 355, the following requirements must be met:

1. *Distribution of stock constituting control.* The parent *(P)* must control the subsidiary *(S)* and distribute all of its stock and securities in *S* or distribute enough stock to constitute control. Section 355(a)(1)(A), (a)(1)(D).
2. *Active business.* Both *P* and *S* must be engaged in the active conduct of a trade or business which has been conducted actively for the five-year period preceding the distribution. Section 355(a)(1)(c), 355(b).
3. *Business purpose.* There must be a business purpose for the distribution. Reg. 1.355-2(c).
4. *The "device" test.* The transaction cannot be used primarily as a device for distributing either *P* or *S*'s earnings and profits. Section 355(a)(1)(B).
5. *Continuity of interest.* There must be a continuity of interest in *P*'s shareholders after the distribution. Section 355(a)(1)(B).

Control is defined in Section 368(c) as the ownership of at least 80 percent of the subsidiary's voting stock and at least 80 percent of the total number of shares of all classes of nonvoting stock. If *P* retains any *S* stock or securities, *P* must satisfy the Treasury that the retention was not pursuant to a plan of tax avoidance. In most cases, *P* may distribute only *S*'s stock or securities tax free. Any other property distributed will be treated as "boot," taxable in accordance with Section 356(b).

According to Section 355, the stock of either an existing subsidiary or a newly created one can qualify for a tax-free spin-off. Furthermore, Section 355 does not require *P* to transfer part of its assets to *S*. But if there is such a transfer, it will constitute a "reorganization" under Section 368(a)(1)(D).

According to the active business requirement of Section 355(b), *P* and *S* must be engaged in the active conduct of a trade or business throughout the five-year period ending on the date of the distribution. If *P* or *S* acquires its business during the five years before the distribution, the acquisition must have been one in which no gain or loss was recognized in whole or in part [Section 355(b)(2)(C)], or the acquisition was not a taxable transaction [Section 355(b)(2)(D)].

The reason for this requirement is to prevent a corporation from investing its surplus funds in a new business or in the stock of a corporation conducting a business and then spinning that stock off rather than paying dividends. If the business has been actively conducted for five years, it is presumed that the acquisition and distribution were not related and that the corporation was not attempting a tax-free separation of liquid assets to avoid taxes on dividends.

What constitutes "active conduct of a trade or business" is not as clear-cut as it might seem. According to Regs. § 1.355-1(c) and Prop. Regs.

§1.355-3(b)(2)(ii), a § 355 "business" must consist of activities that "include every operation which forms a part of, or a step in, the process of earning income or profit," including the collection of income and the payment of expenses. This definition is sufficiently vague to have resulted in numerous interpretive rulings and cases.

If a firm operates a manufacturing, retail, or other business which is five-years old, the business clearly meets the active business requirement of Section 355. But the holding of property or securities for investment purposes does not constitute the active conduct of a trade or business,[5] nor does ownership and operation of land and buildings used in the owner's trade or business.[6] The regulations give three examples of firms engaged in a trade or business that want to separate their real estate holdings from other assets.[7] In one example, the real estate was the factory of a manufacturing corporation, but the regulations stated that the operation of the factory was not separate from the corporation's manufacturing activities. The other two examples involved banks that wanted to spin-off buildings in which their banking operations were conducted. For one bank, ten out of eleven floors of an office building were rented to tenants, while another bank rented only one-half of the second floor of a two-story building. The regulations stated that the first bank's rental activities constituted a trade or business, but the second bank's rental activity was "only incidental to its banking business." Furthermore, according to Prop. Regs. 1.355-3(b)(2), if the property is not actively managed by the owner, which means the owner does not perform significant services related to the operation and management of the leased property, such property cannot be divided under Section 355. The implication, according to Willens (1980), is "if a corporation's trade or business is performed primarily by independent contractors such as rental agents managing an apartment building, the trade or business in question will not be deemed to be actively conducted."[8]

The business purpose requirement, a nonstatutory requirement for the attainment of tax-free status, is that the purpose for the spin-off is germane to the business of the corporations. Not only must there be a business purpose for separating two businesses, but also for distributing the securities to shareholders. If the claimed business purpose can be achieved by separate incorporation of a subsidiary without distributing the subsidiary's stock to *P*'s stockholders, the distribution would not be tax free.[9]

Another aspect of the business purpose requirement is that there must be a corporate purpose rather than a shareholder purpose motivating the spin-off. While this requirement is controversial and subject to differing judicial interpretations, it is clear that the business purpose must be germane to the business of the corporation. A distribution motivated by estate tax planning would not be tax free because it serves a stockholder purpose rather than a corporate purpose. But, if a shareholder purpose and business purpose exist together such that they are indistinguishable, the business purpose requirement will be satisfied.

Proposed Regs. 1.355-2(b)(2) gives four examples of the business purpose test. Examples 1, 2, and 4 found antitrust laws, settling shareholder disputes, and compliance with lender's requirements for financing, respectively, to be valid business purposes. Example 3 involved separating a high-risk business which was not justified because such purpose could be achieved by separate incorporation without distribution to *P*'s stockholders. Other business purposes that might support a tax-free distribution under Section 355 include:

1. Attempt to contain union-organizing activities. See Sidney L. Olson, 48 TC 855 (1967) (Acq.).
2. Expand credit availability for one or both corporations. Rev. Rul. 77-22, 1977-1 CB 91.
3. Separation of a business to permit its employees to share in profits of ownership. Rev. Rul. 69-460.
4. Avoidance of state and local taxes being paid by parent. Rev. Rul. 76-187, 1976-1 CB 97.
5. Remove assets from a foreign country to avoid confiscation. Rev. Rul. 76-187, 1976-1 CB 97.
6. Making *S*'s stock more acceptable in a merger. See Rev. Rul. 76-527, 1976-2 CB 103.
7. Distribution of bank by one-bank holding company to comply with banking requirements. Rev. Rul. 75-321.
8. Distribution of unwanted subsidiary to facilitate *P*'s acquisition of another corporation. Rev. Rul. 72-530.

The "device test" requires that the transaction is not used as a device to effectively distribute earnings or profits of any of the companies involved at capital gains rates rather than at ordinary income rates. An example of a device is where shareholders receive stock in a spin-off and then sell the shares at capital gains rates, with such sales having been negotiated prior to the spin-off.[10]

Prop. Regs. 1.355-2(c) identifies two major factors that must be considered in determining if a device exists: (1) postdistribution stock sales and (2) the nature, kind, amount, and use of the corporation's assets. With regard to postdistribution stock sales, Prop. Regs. 1.355-2(c)(2) considers a prearranged sale of 20 percent or more of the stock of *P* or *S* as a "device" *per se* and would thus make 355 inapplicable. The prearranged sale of less than 20 percent of the stock of *P* or *S* would be viewed as evidence of a device. Any postdistribution sales, even if not prearranged, would also be viewed as evidence of a device. Evidence of a device is subject to refutation.[11] Like other tests previously described, the device test is subject to considerable judicial interpretation. Generally, the problem lies in the nature, kind, amount, and use of the assets of *P, S,* or both.

The proposed regulations identify the following types of situations that might run afoul of the device test.

1. Purchase of a new business within five years of the distribution will be evidence of a device if such business constitutes a significant part of the assets of any spun-off firm. Prop. Regs. § 1.355-2(c)(3).

2. The transfer of liquid assets to S beyond S's reasonable business needs may be problematic. For example, if S is worth $50,000 and holds liquid assets valued at $500,000, an amount that exceeds S's business needs, the Internal Revenue Service might view this spin-off as a device for the distribution of earnings. Reg. § 1.355-2(c)(3).

3. Postdistribution intercorporate transactions can be evidence of a device [Prop. Regs. § 1.333-3(c)]. Example 8 of the proposed regulations, which deals with the separation of the manufacturing and sales functions of a corporation, illustrates this point. If the sales corporation continues to act as the exclusive sales agent for the manufacturing corporation such a separation might be viewed as a device.

With regard to corporate versus shareholder purpose, motives must be germane to the continuance of the corporate purpose for the distribution not to be deemed as a device for distributing earnings and profits or for converting what should have been dividends into capital gains.[12]

The continuity of interest requirement mandates that the transferors retain an interest, such as stock, in the underlying corporate assets, though the shares received need not have voting rights.[13] Application of this requirement is again subject to considerable controversy. An example where the continuity of interest requirement comes into play is when P distributes the stock of S, a newly-formed corporation, to P's stockholders, who immediately dispose of S's stock. If the disposition was prearranged, the IRS would regard the transaction as a sale of P or S's business assets, and a dividend would be taxed at ordinary rates to P's shareholders.[14]

According to Wellen (1980)[15] if S is preexisting, three factors must be present in a disposition of S after the spin-off before the IRS will rule that the distribution is tax free.[16]

1. "Real and meaningful" post spin-off shareholder vote on the disposition of S must occur.

2. The stock of P must be "widely-held," apparently to insure a "real and meaningful" shareholder vote.

3. There must be a separate business purpose of both the spin-off and the disposition.

As is true with the other requirements of Section 355, the complexity of the continuity of interest requirement is such that corporate executives are well advised to seek an advance ruling before proceeding with a spin-off, particularly if a subsequent disposition of P or S is planned.[17]

NOTES

1. If the spin-off does not qualify as tax free under Section 355, the distribution of *S*'s stock or securities to *P*'s shareholders will be treated as an ordinary distribution under Section 301, which is taxable as a dividend. If the spin-off is preceded by a transfer of part of *P*'s assets to *S, P* will recognize neither gain nor loss according to Section 351.

2. The equity method of accounting for investments in common stock is described in APB Opinion No. 18.

3. Section 355 also applies to split-offs and split-ups. Split-offs are nonprorata distributions by *P* of *S* stock to one or more *P* shareholders, in exchange for all or part of their *P* stock. Split-ups are liquidations of *P* involving distributions of stock of different subsidiaries to different shareholders.

4. Robert H. Wellen, "Planning a Tax-Free Corporate Division: How to Avoid Ordinary Income," *Taxation for Accountants* (August 1980): 80-84.

5. Reg. Sec. 1.355-1(c), Prop. Regs. 1.355-3(b)(2iv)(A).

6. 452 F.2d 767.

7. Prop. Regs. § 1.355-3(b)(2).

8. Robert Willens, "Section 355: The Minefield of Subchapter C," *CPA Journal* (March 1980): 23-27.

9. Rev. Rul. 69-460, 1969-2 CB 51.

10. Reg. 1.355-2(b)(1).

11. Rev. Rul. 59-197, 1959-1 CB 77.

12. 452 F.2d 767, 72-1, USTC, 9101, 28 AFTR 2d 71-6110 (CA-1, 1971), cert. den.

13. Reg. 1.368-1(b).

14. Rev. Rul. 70-225.

15. Robert H. Wellen, "How to Qualify a Tax-Free Corporate Division and Avoid 'Bail Out Device' Characterization," *Taxation for Accountants* (September 1980): 144-49.

16. Rev. Rul. 75-406.

17. An excellent discussion of many topics discussed in this chapter is provided in Boris I. Bittker and James S. Eustice, "Corporate Divisions," in *Federal Income Taxation of Corporations and Shareholders*, 4th ed. New York: Warren, Gorham and Lamont, 1979.

Economic Analysis of Spin-Offs

5

Voluntary spin-offs, undertaken for the reasons presented in Chapter 2, are expected to lead to an increase in the values of the parent firm's and spun-off firm's shares. In this chapter, financial data are presented on whether or not the aggregate value of the resulting parts is worth more than the prespin-off whole. There are three principal studies that assess the economic benefits of spin-offs; these studies were written by Oppenheimer and Co. (1981), Kudla and McInish (1983), and Miles and Rosenfeld (1984). Each of these studies will be reviewed in this chapter, in turn.

"THE SUM OF THE PARTS"

Oppenheimer and Co., Inc. initiated a periodic research publication, "The Sum of the Parts," in response to the proliferation of spin-offs that has occurred in recent years. The Oppenheimer service covers selected new spin-off situations as they are announced. Included are the details of the spin-off and a monitoring of financial performance, whenever possible, for six to nine months after the spin-off. Although the service does not recommend purchase or sale of specific securities, it does alert the reader to new investment opportunities. For more information, write to Mr. Robert Gordon (212-825-4000), Customer Arbitrage Department, Oppenheimer and Co., Inc., One New York Plaza, New York, New York, 10004.

In one edition, Oppenheimer analyzed financial data for nineteen major spin-offs that occurred in the past decade (one involved the spin-off of two firms simultaneously); a copy of the resulting report is reproduced in Table

5.1. Absolute and relative price performances are presented for the period from the announcement of the spin-off until the spin-off date and also from the spin-off date to six months after the spin-off. Table 5.1 shows that in the large majority of cases the combined value of the parent and spun-off firm after the spin-off was greater than for the parent firm prior to the spin-off. Of the nineteen spin-offs, sixteen increased in value from the announcement date to the spin-off date, one declined in value, and two were approximately unchanged. But for the six months following the spin-off, considering the combined performance of the parent and spun-off firm, only eleven of the spin-offs had increased in value from the spin-off date while eight had declined in value. Nevertheless, the value of the port-folios held by investors six months after the spin-off was still greater than at the date of the spin-off announcement.

Table 5.1 also shows the relative performance of these spin-offs from the stockholders' viewpoint. Relative performance is measured by comparing the performance of the spun-off shares (or prior to the spin-off, the shares of the parent firm) with the performance of the S & P 400 index over a simi-lar time period. The S & P 400 index is a composite index of 400 common stocks compiled by the Standard & Poor's Corporation. It provides a useful benchmark for judging the performance of a portfolio consisting of shares in the parent firm and spun-off firm. The absolute performance of the shares of the firms involved in the spin-off is calculated by dividing the ter-minal value of the investment at the date of interest by the initial value. The absolute performance of the S & P 400 index is calculated in a similar way. Then the relative performance of the value of the shares involved in the spin-off is calculated by dividing the absolute performance measure for the spun-off firms by the absolute performance measure for the S & P 400 in-dex. Fifteen of the nineteen spin-offs showed performance in excess of the S & P 400 index from the announcement date to the spin-off date, while fourteen showed performance in excess of the S & P 400 index from the an-nouncement date to a date six months after the spin-off. Table 5.2 (also re-produced from an Oppenheimer report) examines the performance of a portfolio assuming that $1,000 was invested in each of the spun-off firms at the date of the spin-off. If this portfolio had been held until January 14, 1981, the entire portfolio would have appreciated 440 percent. Had 100 shares of each entity been purchased instead of an equal dollar amount, the percentage gain would have been 243 percent. In summary, Tables 5.1 and 5.2 clearly illustrate that stockholders reaped impressive dollar gains from these spin-offs.

THE KUDLA AND MCINISH STUDY

Kudla and McInish examined the capital market's reaction to six major corporate spin-offs. The identity of each parent and subsidiary firm in-

Table 3.1

Oppenheimer & Company, Inc., *The Sum of the Parts*

EXHIBIT 1

TICKER	NAME	ANNOUNCED DATE	ANNOUNCED VALUE	SPIN-OFF DATE	SPIN-OFF VALUE	% CHANGE	ABS. PERF	REL. PERF	VALUE 6 MOS. AFTER SPIN-OFF	% CHANGE	ABS. PERF	REL. PERF
	S & P 400											
CGP	COASTAL CORP	11/29/79	119.39	1/ 2/80	118.41	-.82	99.18		130.13	9.00	109.00	
VLO	VALERO CORP	11/29/79	32.50	1/ 2/80	22.00				27.25			
		11/29/79	.00	1/ 2/80	11.00				24.38			
	TOTAL DEAL:		32.50		33.00	1.54	101.54	102.38	51.63	58.85	158.85	145.74
	S & P 400											
SFE	SAFEGUARD INDS INC	6/18/79	112.68	3/ 5/80	126.56	12.32	112.32		141.71	25.76	125.76	
SGB	SAFEGUARD BUSINESS SYS INC	6/18/79	16.63	3/ 5/80	5.50				4.63			
		6/18/79	.00	3/ 5/80	24.00				30.75			
	TOTAL DEAL:		16.63		29.50	77.44	177.44	157.98	35.38	112.78	212.78	169.19
	S & P 400											
MSA	MESA PETE CO	6/21/79	113.30	11/19/79	116.91	3.19	103.19		120.77	6.59	106.59	
MESA-O	MESA RTY TR	6/21/79	54.25	11/19/79	46.38				59.75			
		6/21/79	.00	11/19/79	30.25				37.00			
	TOTAL DEAL:		54.25		76.63	41.25	141.25	136.88	96.75	78.34	178.34	167.31
	S & P 400											
REL	RELIANCE GROUP INC	12/ 7/78	107.81	5/14/79	109.40	1.47	101.47		115.90	7.50	107.50	
LEAS	LEASCO CORP (1 FOR 6)	12/ 7/78	36.13	5/14/79	36.50				46.25			
		12/ 7/78	.00	5/14/79	2.98				4.54			
	TOTAL DEAL:		36.13		39.48	9.28	109.28	107.70	50.79	40.60	140.60	130.78
	S & P 400											
IAC	TANDYCRAFTS INC	5/23/78	108.47	4/10/79	115.34	6.33	106.33		118.02	8.81	108.81	
TILE	COLOR TILE INC	5/23/78	18.50	4/10/79	4.75				4.63			
		5/23/78	.00	4/10/79	23.75				30.75			
	TOTAL DEAL:		18.50		28.50	54.05	154.05	144.88	35.38	91.22	191.22	175.74
	S & P 400											
GOI	GEARHART IND	9/21/77	104.64	6/20/78	106.65	1.92	101.92		105.45	.77	100.77	
PGO	PENGO INDS INC (1 FOR 2)	9/21/77	35.00	6/20/78	51.38				66.50			
		9/21/77	.00	6/20/78	3.13				3.94			
	TOTAL DEAL:		35.00		54.50	51.39	151.39	148.54	70.44	95.66	195.66	194.16
	S & P 400											
CLE	COLE NATL CORP	8/1/77	107.57	3/23/78	98.19	-8.72	91.28		112.81	4.87	104.87	
COLE	COLE CONSUMER PRODS INC	8/1/77	10.75	3/23/78	12.75				15.25			
	(1 FOR 2)	8/1/77	.00	3/23/78	2.44				3.31			
	TOTAL DEAL:		10.75		15.19	41.28	141.28	154.77	18.56	72.67	172.67	164.65

Source: Extract from "The Sum of the Parts . . . ," January 14, 1981, Oppenheimer & Co., Inc. Reprinted with permission.

Table 5.1 (continued)
Oppenheimer & Company, Inc., The Sum of the Parts

EXHIBIT I cont'd.

TICKER	NAME	ANN. DATE	ANN. VALUE	SPIN-OFF DATE	SPIN-OFF VALUE	% CHANGE	ABS. PERF	REL. PERF	VALUE 6 MOS. AFTER SPIN-OFF	% CHANGE	ABS. PERF	REL. PERF
	S & P 400		111.66		112.17	.46	100.46		102.97	-7.78	92.22	
TYL	TYLER CORP	2/22/77	21.88	4/15/77	22.75				20.63			
CRNS	CRONUS INDS INC	2/22/77	.00	4/15/77	1.21				1.83			
	(1 FOR 3)	2/22/77		4/15/77								
	TOTAL DEAL:		21.88		23.96	9.52	109.52	109.02	22.46	2.67	102.67	111.33
	S & P 400		115.15		110.23	-4.27	95.73		101.97	-11.45	88.55	
OXM	OXFORD INDS INC	1/19/77	26.63	7/ 5/77	7.88				10.75			
LBP	LANIER BUSINESS PRODS INC	1/19/77	.10	7/ 5/77	26.44				32.63			
	(3 FOR 2)	1/19/77		7/ 5/77								
	TOTAL DEAL:		26.73		34.31	28.38	128.38	134.11	43.38	62.28	162.28	183.26
	S & P 400		111.55		119.46	7.09	107.09		110.25	-1.16	98.84	
REFC	REFAC TECHNOLOGY DEV CORP	11/15/76	3.25	1/ 1/77	3.75				9.62			
SCMA	SCRIPTOMATIC INC	11/15/76	.42	1/ 1/77	.58				2.25			
	(2 FOR 3)	11/15/76		1/ 1/77								
	TOTAL DEAL:		3.67		4.33	18.17	118.17	110.35	11.87	223.80	323.80	327.62
	S & P 400		116.42		113.49	-2.52	97.48		111.56	-4.17	95.83	
BFI	BROWNING FERRIS INDS INC	6/28/76	7.50	10/18/76	6.13				9.88			
CFIB	CONSOLIDATED FIBRES INC	6/28/76	.00	10/18/76	.29				.34			
	(1 FOR 10)	6/28/76		10/18/76								
	TOTAL DEAL:		7.50		6.41	-14.50	85.50	87.71	10.21	36.17	136.17	142.10
	S & P 400		113.21		116.47	2.88	102.88		119.46	5.52	105.52	
WB	WACHOVIA CORP	4/18/76	26.50	7/ 1/76	22.88				21.00			
ACR	AMERICAN CR CORP	4/18/76	.00	7/ 1/76	4.71				5.71			
	(1 FOR 3)	4/18/76		7/ 1/76								
	TOTAL DEAL:		26.50		27.58	4.09	104.09	101.17	26.71	.79	100.79	95.51
	S & P 400		111.00		113.92	2.63	102.63		110.75	-.23	99.77	
TAC	TANDYCRAFTS INC	1/27/76	19.00	5/14/76	17.25				12.88			
SLI	STAFFORD LOWDON CO	1/27/76	.00	5/14/76	1.69				1.13			
	(1 FOR 4)	1/27/76		5/14/76								
	TOTAL DEAL:		19.00		18.94	-.33	99.67	97.12	14.00	-26.32	73.68	73.85
	S & P 400		101.82		102.19	.36	100.36		112.68	10.67	110.67	
TAN	TANDY CORP	5/27/75	38.50	11/28/75	46.62				73.25			
TAC	TANDYCRAFTS INC	5/27/75	.00	11/28/75	7.06				7.75			
	(1 FOR 2)	5/27/75		11/28/75								
TAB	TANDY BRANDS INC	5/27/75	.00	11/28/75	.75				1.14			
	(1 FOR 10)											
	TOTAL DEAL:		38.50		54.44	41.38	141.38	140.87	82.14	113.32	213.32	192.76

EXHIBIT 1 cont'd.

Table 5.1 *(continued)*
Oppenheimer & Company, Inc., *The Sum of the Parts*

TICKER	NAME	ANNOUNCED DATE	ANNOUNCED VALUE	SPIN-OFF DATE	SPIN-OFF VALUE	% CHANGE	ABS. PERF	REL. PERF	VALUE 6 MOS. AFTER SPIN-OFF	% CHANGE	ABS. PERF	REL. PERF
	S & P 400	1/ 6/75	78.89	6/30/75	106.86	35.45	135.45		133.75	27.34	127.34	
ANR	AMERICAN NAT RES CO	1/ 6/75	36.37	6/30/75	35.12				33.75			
WIC	WICOR INC	1/ 6/75	.79	6/30/75	3.75				3.40			
	(1 FOR 5)											
	TOTAL DEAL:		37.17		38.87	4.59	104.59	77.21	37.15	-.05	99.95	78.49
	S & P 400	3/14/74	111.55	4/16/74	104.98	-5.89	94.11		78.46	-29.66	70.34	
PZL	PENNZOIL CO	3/14/74	26.63	4/16/74	26.88				16.12			
UER	UNITED ENERGY RES INC	3/14/74	.00	4/16/74	1.95				1.65			
	(3 FOR 10)											
	TOTAL DEAL:		26.63		28.83	8.26	108.26	115.04	17.77	-33.24	66.76	94.91
	S & P 400	9/25/73	121.30	5/ 1/74	103.97	-14.29	85.71		82.71	-31.81	68.19	
ELG	EL PASO CO	9/25/73	14.50	5/ 1/74	13.00				10.63			
NWP	NORTHWEST ENERGY CO	9/25/73	.00	5/ 1/74	1.61				1.50			
	(1 FOR 10)											
	TOTAL DEAL:		14.50		14.61	.78	100.78	117.57	12.12	-16.38	83.62	122.63
	S & P 400	7/24/72	120.81	12/29/72	131.87	9.15	109.15		116.72	-3.39	96.61	
GP	GEORGIA PAC CORP	7/24/72	40.07	12/29/72	36.94				32.57			
LPX	LOUISIANA PAC CORP	7/24/72	.00	12/29/72	6.51				6.00			
	(1 FOR 4)											
	TOTAL DEAL:		40.07		43.45	8.42	108.42	99.33	38.57	-3.75	96.25	99.62
	S & P 400	6/29/70	80.09	6/ 4/71	112.12	39.99	139.99		107.28	33.95	133.95	
CBS	CBS INC	6/29/70	27.25	6/ 4/71	46.63				44.75			
VIA	VIACOM INTL INC OHIO	6/29/70	.00	6/ 4/71	2.58				1.94			
	(100 FOR 714)											
	TOTAL DEAL:		27.25		49.21	80.58	180.58	128.99	46.69	71.35	171.35	127.92

DEFINITIONS :
DATE ANNOUNCED - DATE SPIN-OFF WAS FIRST PUBLICLY PROPOSED.
% CHANGE - % CHANGE OF VALUE FROM DATE ANNOUNCED TO SPIN-OFF DATE AND
FROM DATE ANNOUNCED TO SIX MONTHS AFTER SPIN-OFF DATE.
ABSOLUTE PERFORMANCE - PERFORMANCE ASSUMING A VALUE OF 100 AT DATE OF ANNOUNCEMENT.
RELATIVE PERFORMANCE - PERFORMANCE RELATIVE TO S & P 400; 100 IS EQUAL TO THE PERFORMANCE OF THE MARKET.
TOTAL DEAL - VALUE OF A SINGLE SHARE OF PARENT AT DATE OF SPIN-OFF AND EACH VALUATION DATE, ADJUSTED FOR
SPIN-OFF RATIO, STOCK SPLITS AND STOCK DIVIDENDS.

Table 5.2

Oppenheimer & Company, Inc., The Sum of the Parts

<pre>
EXHIBIT II   OPPENHEIMER & CO., INC.   1/ 6/81

                MODEL SPIN-OFF PORTFOLIO *

                                                              SPIN-OFF S&P 400
                                      SPIN-OFF   ORIGINAL S&P 400 CURRENT   %   %   ABS.   REL.
TICKER   NAME   DATE   INVESTMENT VALUE   VALUE   CHANGE   CHANGE   PERF.   PERF.
------- ------------------------   --------   ---------- ------- --------   ------- ------ ------- -------
VLO   VALERO CORP   1/ 2/80 $ 1000.00 118.41 $3465.91   246.59   32.61   346.59   261.37
SGB   SAFEGUARD BUSINESS SYS INC   3/ 5/80   1000.00 126.56   1406.25   40.62   24.07   140.62   113.35
MESA-0   MESA RTY TR   11/19/79   1000.00 116.91   1239.67   23.97   34.31   123.97   92.30
LEAS   LEASCO CORP   5/14/79   1000.00 109.40   3076.92   207.69   43.53   307.69   214.38
TILE   COLOR TILE INC   4/10/79   1000.00 115.34   2121.09   112.11   36.14   212.11   155.80
PGO   PENGO INDS INC   6/20/78   1000.00 106.65   4620.00   362.00   47.23   462.00   313.79
COLE   COLE CONSUMER PRODS INC   3/23/78   1000.00   98.19   2307.69 (A) 130.77   59.92   230.77   144.31
CRNS   CRONUS INDS INC   4/15/77   1000.00 112.17   1603.59   60.36   39.99   160.36   114.55
LBP   LANIER BUSINESS PRODS INC   7/ 5/77   1000.00 110.23   3148.67   214.87   42.45   314.87   221.04
SCMA   SCRIPTOMATIC INC   1/ 1/77   1000.00 119.46 30718.32 (B) 2971.83 31.44 3071.83 2337.01
CFIB   CONSOLIDATED FIBRES INC   10/18/76   1000.00 113.49   3413.22   241.32   38.36   341.32   246.70
ACR   AMERICAN CR CORP   7/ 1/76   1000.00 116.47   3539.82 (C) 253.98   34.82   353.98   262.56
SLI   STAFFORD LOWDON CO   5/14/76   1000.00 113.92   3962.96 (D) 296.30   37.83   396.30   287.52
TAC   TANDYCRAFTS INC   11/28/75   1000.00 102.19   4623.87 (E) 362.39   53.66   462.39   300.92
TAB   TANDY BRANDS INC   11/28/75   1000.00 102.19   8800.00   780.00   53.66   880.00   572.71
WIC   WICOR INC   6/30/75   1000.00 106.86   1080.00   8.00   46.94   108.00   73.50
UER   UNITED ENERGY RES INC   4/16/74   1000.00 104.98 17771.04   1677.14   49.57 1777.14 1188.15
NWP   NORTHWEST ENERGY CO   5/ 1/74   1000.00 103.97   5906.98   490.70   51.03   590.70   391.12
LPX   LOUISIANA PAC CORP   12/29/72   1000.00 131.87   2195.16   119.52   19.07   219.52   184.36
VIA   VIACOM INTL INC OHIO   6/ 4/71   1000.00 112.12   3091.52   209.15   40.05   309.15   220.75
                                     ---------- ----------   -------
                          TOTALS : $ 20000.00 $ 108092.80   440.46% (F)
</pre>

* THIS PORTFOLIO ASSUMES AN INVESTMENT OF $1,000 IN EACH SPIN-OFF ENTITY
  ON THE DATE OF SPIN-OFF. THESE POSITIONS ARE ADJUSTED FOR ALL SUBSEQUENT
  STOCK SPLITS AND STOCK DIVIDENDS. IN THOSE CASES WHERE A SUBSEQUENT
  MERGER TOOK PLACE, THE CURRENT VALUE REPRESENTS THE VALUE ON THE
  DATE OF THE MERGER.

(A) COLE - 3/30/80 MERGED AT $11.25 PER SHARE INTO SHELTER RESOURCES CORP.
(B) SCMA - 9/19/80 MERGED AT $16.25 PER SHARE INTO BRITISH ELECTRIC CO.
(C) ACR - 5/23/79 MERGED AT $50.00 PER SHARE INTO BARCLAY'S BANK
                   INTERNATIONAL LTD.
(D) SLI - 9/13/79 MERGED AT $26.75 PER SHARE INTO AMERICAN STANDARD INC.
(E) TANDYCRAFTS CURRENT VALUE INCLUDES COLOR TILE AND STAFFORD LOWDON
                   WHICH WERE BOTH SUBSEQUENTLY SPUN-OFF.
(F) AN INVESTMENT OF 100 SHARES IN EACH SPIN-OFF ENTITY WOULD HAVE RESULTED
    IN A % GAIN OF 234%.

Source: Extract from "The Sum of the Parts . . . ," January 14, 1981, Oppenheimer & Co.,
Inc. Reprinted with permission.

volved in these spin-offs and related information are listed in Table 5.3.
Notice that the size of the spin-offs ranged from 6 percent to 47 percent of
the parent firm's assets. Accordingly, these spin-offs were significant financial events that could easily have an impact on stockholders' wealth.
Because it seems likely that corporate management would not undertake a
voluntary spin-off unless they expected it to be beneficial, Kudla and
McInish hypothesized that the market should react positively to that information, resulting in an increase in shareholder wealth.

The "residual analysis" technique developed by Fama, Fisher, Jensen
and Roll (1969) was used to investigate whether these spin-offs resulted in
increased shareholder wealth. The advantage of this technique is that it
automatically controls for both movements in the stock market during the
period around the spin-off date, and for differential risk associated with
each firm. The primary control for the market effect comes from netting
out the return on the market. Market effects are also controlled to some ex-

Table 5.3
Sample Characteristics

Parent Firm	Spun-Off Firm	Size of Spin-Off[a] (Percent)	Approximate Date of Spin-Off
Browning-Ferris Industries	Consolidated Fibres	22	September 24, 1976
Easco Corp.	Eastmet Corp.	47	December 1, 1972
Olin Corp.	Olinkraft Corp.	12	June 7, 1974
Tandy Corp.	Tandycraft, Inc.	18	October 24, 1975
Tandy Corp.	Tandy Brands	6	October 24, 1975
Valmac Corp.	Distribuco, Inc.	10	July 27, 1973

Source: "Valuation Consequences of Corporate Spin-Offs," *Review of Business and Economic Research,* March 1983: 71-77. Reprinted with permission.

[a]Spun-off firm as a percent of total assets of parent firm before the spin-off.

tent by averaging over widely disparate time periods such as those listed in Table 5.3. Residuals were estimated from equation (1):

$$\tilde{R}_{jt} = \alpha_j + \beta_j\tilde{R}_{mt} + \varepsilon_{jt} \tag{1}$$

where

$\tilde{R}_{jt}$ is the return on security j in week t consisting of capital gains yield plus dividend yield adjusted for stock splits and stock dividends.

α_j and β_j = parameters to be estimated.

$\tilde{R}_{mt}$ = return on Standard & Poor's 500 Index defined as $(P_{mt+1} - P_{mt})/P_{mt}$ where P_{mt} are week end prices for S & P 500.

ε_{jt} = the residual return on security j for week t.

and the tildes indicate random variables. The analysis focuses on ε_{jt} because the residual return represents that portion of the security's weekly return which is not related to the return on the market. These residual returns were examined to determine whether or not they were affected by the spin-offs. To reduce any bias in the estimates of α_j and β_j and because of missing return data (in the Standard and Poor's *Daily Stock Price Record),* a total of twelve weeks surrounding the spin-off week (six weeks before and six weeks after) were eliminated from the analysis.

The parameters α_j and β_j were estimated by regressing security returns on market returns as described in equation (1) for sixty weeks before and sixty weeks after the spin-off. Designating the spin-off week as week 0, the prespin-off subsample consists of weeks -66 to -7. The postspin-off subsample consists of weeks $+7$ to $+66$. For the prespin-off regression analysis, the returns for the parent firms were used. A weighted portfolio of returns for the parent firm and the spun-off firm was used in the postspin-off analysis. The weights were based on the number of shares of the spun-off firm that the parent firm's stockholders received. For example, Valmac stockholders received one share of Distribuco for each three shares of Valmac stock held. Therefore, the weighted portfolio comprised three shares of Valmac and one share of Distribuco.

The weekly residuals for all six firms were averaged in an attempt to avoid the effects of other firm-specific events which might have influenced a particular firm's weekly residual returns. A positive residual for any week indicates performance greater than expected given the risk class of the firm and the return on the market; a negative residual indicates performance less than expected given the risk class of the firm and the return on the market. Weekly average residuals for week m were defined as follows:

$$\varepsilon_m = \sum_{j=1}^{6} \varepsilon_{jm/6} \quad m = -66 \text{ to } -7 \text{ and } +7 \text{ to } +66 \qquad (2)$$

A visual interpretation of the market's reaction to the spin-off is provided in Figure 5.1. Figure 5.1. shows the cumulative average residuals for each week from relative week -46 to -7 and $+7$ to $+46$. The cumulative residuals for each week m were computed from the weekly average residuals as follows:

$$E_m = \sum_{j=-46}^{m} \bar{\varepsilon}_j \quad \begin{array}{l} m = -46 \text{ to } +46 \\ \text{excluding } -6 \text{ to } +6 \end{array} \qquad (3)$$

If there is no market reaction to the spin-offs, then E_m would be expected to fluctuate randomly about zero. Whenever the line is upward sloping, performance of the spun-off firm's shares was "in excess" of expectations given the risk class of the firm and the movement of the market; a downward sloping line indicates performance less that expected given the risk class of the firm and the movement of the market. Note that a "favorable" price movement is defined relative to the market. Thus, if the market goes down and the stock goes down this could be a favorable movement as long as the stock went down less than expected.

Other things being equal, the market's reaction is expected to result in a positive impact on stock prices (i.e., positive returns) because the separate firms are expected to be more valuable than when they were combined. In all cases but one, the actual announcement of the spin-off as reported in the *Wall Street Journal* occurred 16-20 weeks before the spin-off took place. An inspection of Figure 5.1 indicates that the cumulative average residuals fluctuate randomly from week (relative to the spin-off week, week 0) -46 to -40, but then rise sharply from week -40, reaching a peak at week -15. Subsequently, E_m appears to fluctuate randomly.

The fact that the risk-adjusted returns on the parent firms exceeded the market returns in the period preceding the spin-off suggests that the spin-offs were anticipated by the market. To determine if these excess returns were statistically significant, a t-test was performed on the average residuals from weeks -40 to -15. The computed t statistic of 1.63 was significant at the 10 percent level (25 degrees of freedom).

The market's reaction to the spin-off appeared to be impounded in the stock prices of the parent firms by the time the spin-off was announced about 16-20 weeks prior to the actual spin-offs.

In summary, the residual analysis indicated that the spin-offs did have a material positive impact on stock returns. In addition, the market began to anticipate the spin-offs forty weeks prior to the spin-off dates.

THE MILES AND ROSENFELD STUDY

Miles and Rosenfeld (1984) examined the effect of spin-offs on shareholder wealth for a sample of 59 companies that had engaged in a spin-off during the 1963-1980 period. First, using daily stock returns (dividends plus capital gains, before taxes), they estimated daily abnormal returns which were equal to the difference between observed returns and predicted returns.

Miles and Rosenfeld used the mean adjusted return model (or comparison period approach) as developed by Brown and Warner. Specifically, the abnormal daily returns for each security were computed by subtracting the security's average daily return over the comparison period from its actual daily return over the observation period. The observation period was 121 trading days surrounding and including day 0 (i.e., day -60 through day $+60$), where day 0 is the day the spin-off was announced in the *Wall Street Journal*. The comparison period is the average daily return from day -240 through day -61, for a total of 180 trading days.

Second, the abnormal returns were averaged each day across all companies in the sample during the observation period. These average returns were then cumulated over a specified time period to assess the abnormal price behavior of the sample securities attributable to the public announcement of the spin-offs. Miles and Rosenfeld compared the performance of

Figure 5.1
Plot of Cumulative Residuals for Six Voluntary Corporate Spin-Offs

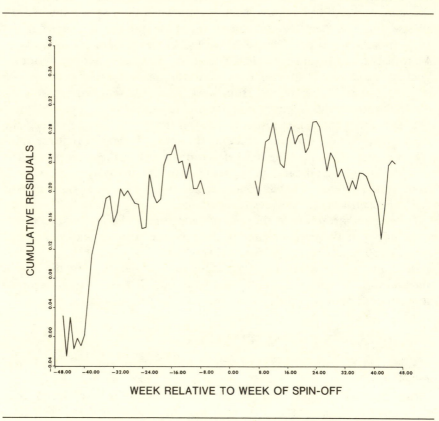

WEEK RELATIVE TO WEEK OF SPIN-OFF

Source: "Valuation Consequences of Corporate Spin-Offs," *Review of Business and Economic Research,* March 1983: 71-77. Reprinted with permission.

large and small spin-offs. A large spin-off was defined as one in which the spun-off firm had an equity market value of at least 10 percent as large as the market value of the parent firm's common stock. Small spin-offs had a market value less than 10 percent of the parent's equity value. Of the 59 spin-offs in the sample, 38 were classified as large while 21 were designated as small.

Statistical tests applied to the average and cumulative abnormal returns for a subsample of large spin-offs, and small spin-offs indicated that the large spin-offs had a significant positive impact on shareholder wealth while the small spin-offs did not have a significant impact. Of course, this does not necessarily mean that small spin-offs did not increase shareholder wealth. Instead, it is more likely that any increase in wealth resulting from small spin-offs was simply not detected due to its being overshadowed by other factors.

Miles and Rosenfeld also found that the news of the spin-offs appeared to be impounded in security prices within five trading days after the event, indicating that the market responded rapidly to the publicly available information. There was also evidence that the market anticipated the spin-off announcement.

Miles and Rosenfeld provided evidence that the positive impact on shareholder wealth of large voluntary spin-offs is partially due to the wealth transfer effect. The wealth transfer effect results from wealth being transferred from bondholders to stockholders because bondholders can no longer rely on the cash flow from the subsidiary to support debt payments. Thus, after the spin-off, the parent firm's bondholders no longer have a claim on the subsidiary's cash flows, which reduces the value of the bonds and, consequently, increases the wealth of the parent firm's shareholders by a similar amount.

Stockholders may also benefit from transfers of wealth from holders of securities other than bonds. An excellent example is the spin-off of Leasco Corporation from Reliance Group mentioned in Chapter 3. Reliance concluded that its preferred stockholders and warrant holders (as well as its convertible bond holders) were entitled to notice of the spin-off, but that "no adjustment in the terms or in the current conversion or exercise prices of these securities is required by reason of the dividend of the Leasco Common Stock, and holders of these securities can only receive such dividend if they convert their securities into, or exercise their rights to acquire, as the case may be, Reliance Group common stock prior to the Record Date." (See Leasco Corporation Prospectus, April 4, 1979, p. 8.) Thus, following the spin-off, an increase in the wealth of Reliance stockholders at the expense of the other security holders of Reliance could be expected.

Another reason for the favorable performance of firms' share prices following a spin-off is the information content of the spin-off. According to Miles and Rosenfeld, firms with multiple lines of business are difficult to value because of a lack of accounting data and because few analysts track (or fully understand) multiple-industry firms. A spin-off will enable investors to better evaluate the individual lines of business, thus increasing shareholder wealth.

Miles and Rosenfeld also compared the performance of voluntary and involuntary spin-offs. Results indicated that the voluntary spin-offs had a positive and statistically significant impact on shareholder wealth, while the involuntary spin-offs had a negative (but statistically insignificant) impact on shareholder wealth. These authors speculated that the negative impact of involuntary spin-offs may result from loss of synergies that existed prior to the spin-off due to the coordinated efforts of the parent and subsidiary. Chapter 7 describes the involuntary spin-off of Louisiana-Pacific Corporation by Georgia-Pacific Corporation. Results of the analysis presented in Chapter 7 showed a significant negative impact on shareholder wealth.

This chapter reviewed three studies which have examined the effects of spin-offs on shareholder wealth. These studies used very different methodologies; two were written by academicians, while one was written by brokers. Despite these differences, the studies agree that, in general, voluntary corporate spin-offs have increased stockholder wealth. As one might have expected, the impact of large spin-offs on stockholder wealth was greater than that of small spin-offs. Several reasons which could, at least partially, explain the increase in stockholder wealth resulting from the spin-off were discussed. These included wealth transfers from other security holders and the information content of the spin-off announcement. Spin-offs appeared to have been anticipated by the stock market as much as forty weeks before their announcement. In contrast, involuntary spin-offs were found to have a negative impact on stockholder wealth.

REFERENCES

Stephen Brown and Jerold Warner, "Measuring Security Price Performance," *Journal of Financial Economics* 8 (September 1980): 205-58.

Eugene Fama, Lawrence Fisher, Michael Jensen, and Richard Roll, "The Adjustment of Stock Prices to New Information," *International Economic Review* 10 (February 1969): 1-21.

Ronald J. Kudla and Thomas H. McInish, "Valuation Consequences of Corporate Spin-Offs," *Review of Business and Economic Research,* March 1983: 71-77.

James A. Miles and James D. Rosenfeld, "An Empirical Analysis of the Effects of Spin-Off Announcements on Shareholder Wealth," *The Journal of Finance,* Vol. 38, No. 5 (December 1983): 1597-1606.

Tandy Corporation:
Case Study

6

This chapter is divided into three sections. First, a brief history of Tandy Corporation and a description of the company's divestiture program is provided. Then, the criteria used by Tandy management to decide between a sale and a spin-off are outlined. The final section reviews the perceived benefits of spin-offs.

Much of the following presentation is based on discussions with G. R. Nugent, Chairman, President and Chief Executive Officer of Tandycrafts, Inc., and William H. Michero, Senior Vice President and Secretary of Tandycrafts. Both Mr. Nugent and Mr. Michero have been officers of Tandy Corporation and/or Tandycrafts for more than twenty years. Mr. Nugent became President at the time of the spin-off of Color Tile by Tandycrafts; he came from Tandy Corporation where he was Vice President and also Executive Vice President of its Radio Shack Division. Mr. Michero has been an officer of Tandycrafts since its spin-off from Tandy Corporation.

BACKGROUND

In 1959, a group of Texans led by Charles D. Tandy took control of General American Industries, Inc. and, shortly thereafter, changed the name of the firm to Tandy Corporation. During the following decade, a large number of acquisitions were made including the Radio Shack Co., which later became the principal component of the business. By 1970, Tandy Corporation operated thirty-seven different businesses. It was about this time that management began to recognize the difficulties of managing a conglomerate enterprise and began to think about streamlining operations through divestitures and spin-offs. Management recognized the outstanding potential of the Radio Shack business and advantages (discussed below) of separating it from the conglomerate.

In the period 1974-1982, a number of sales and spin-offs were completed. Table 6.1 indicates the principal businesses of Tandy Corporation in 1974 and their subsequent disposition. Eleven businesses were transferred to Tandycrafts, Inc. and spun off in October 1975. An additional six businesses were transferred to Tandy Brands, Inc. and also spun off in October 1975. Tandy Corporation sold the businesses comprising the General Retailing Group, as well as Allied Electronics and Corral Sportswear.

Following the spin-off, Tandycrafts began its own sale/spin-off program. Stafford-Lowdon and Color Tile were spun off in 1976 and 1979, respectively. Royal Tile, Decorating and Crafts Magazine, Woodie Taylor Vending, and Automated and Custom Food Service were sold in 1975.

CRITERIA FOR SPIN-OFFS

According to Mr. Michero, the number one rule in undertaking a spin-off is the welfare and benefit of the continuing shareholders. These are the shareholders who have been with you for some time and will stay with you. A spin-off should not be undertaken at the insistence of "the hot money crowd."

Table 6.2 presents a checklist of important characteristics of a business which should be considered in deciding between a sale or spin-off. If a firm is to be spun off, it must be of sufficient size and have sufficient financial resources to survive; hence, the first two items. The next two items in Table 6.2 reflect the growth philosophy of Tandy companies. Why sell a firm to someone else if its current management is capable of achieving rapid and profitable growth? Such a company might be called "buildable." A company is buildable if it earns sufficient return and operates in a market with sufficient growth opportunities. The final two items in Table 6.2 pertain to the potential market for the firm. If there is an anxious buyer, the chance of getting a favorable price is enhanced, which would, of course, increase the desirability of sale. When there is difficulty in valuating a business, it *may* be desirable to spin that business off rather than sell the business. But probably it should be pointed out that capital markets also have difficulty in valuing some types of firms, such as those with substantial real estate assets.

Insight into the application of the items in Table 6.2 might result from a closer examination of the sales and spin-offs enumerated in Table 6.1. During 1974 and 1975, Tandy sold or liquidated the companies comprising its General Retailing Group. An important reason that these businesses were sold rather than spun off was lack of positive cash flow. In fiscal 1973, the

Table 6.1

*Divestitures and Major Continuing Operations of Tandy Corporation
and Successors, 1974-1982*

Tandy Corporation	Status
Radio Shack Division	Continuing
General Retailing Group	
Leonards Department Stores	Sold March 1974
Mitchells of Fort Worth	Discontinued 1974
Wolfe Nurseries	Sold March 1975
Leonards Auto Centers	Sold June 1975
Corral Sportswear Company	Sold May 1975
Allied Electronics, Inc.	Sold March 1978
Tandycrafts, Inc.	**Spun-off Oct. 1975**
Tandy Leather	Continuing
Magee	Continuing
Decorating and Crafts Magazine	Sold August 1975
Royal Tile	Sold late 1975
Woodie Taylor Vending	Sold December 1975
Automated and Custom Food Service	Sold December 1975
Stafford-Lowdon	Spun-off March 1976
Color Tile	Spun-off March 1979
American Handicrafts	Discontinued 1982
Merribee	Discontinued 1982
Bona Allen, Inc.	Destroyed (fire) 1982
Tandy Brands, Inc.	**Spun-off Oct. 1975**
Collins of Texas	Continuing
Hickok Manufacturing Co.	Continuing
J. M. Bucheimer	Continuing
Tex Tan Welhausen	Continuing
Tex Tan Western	Continuing
Western Sales	Continuing

Source: Annual reports of Tandy Corporation, Tandycrafts, Inc., and Tandy Brands, Inc.

General Retailing Group had losses of $4.1 million on sales of $63 million. Hence, the viability of these businesses as separate entities was uncertain. A second important factor was that these businesses were not buildable. For example, at the end of fiscal 1973 the Mitchells, Inc. chain operated 74 stores, an increase of 63 units during the previous four years. But this rapid growth in size had not been accompanied by a correspondingly rapid growth in profits. Consequently, management found it necessary to slow the pace of expansion in order to place increased emphasis on the development of profitability.

Table 6.2
Spin-Off versus Sale

Characteristics of Business	Answer Associated with	
	Spin-Off	Sale
Large Size	Yes	No
Positive Cash Flow	Yes	No
Buildable	Yes	No
Aggressive Management	Yes	No
Anxious Buyer	No	Yes
Difficult to Value	Yes	No

Despite the fact that the companies comprising the General Retailing Group were unprofitable and unbuildable in the hands of Tandy management, there were buyers available. The Mitchells and Leonards divisions were sold for $5.4 million in cash, $2.3 million in notes and accounts receivable, and 334,445 shares of Dillard Department Stores, Inc. class "A" common stock (with a market value in June 1975 of $4.5 million). In addition, Wolfe Nurseries was sold to Pier 1 Imports. Hence, the sale of these subsidiaries raised substantial funds which could be redirected into more profitable growth opportunities.

In contrast to its General Retailing Group, which was sold, Tandy Corporation spun off its Tandycrafts and Tandy Brands subsidiaries. For fiscal 1975, sales of Tandycrafts were $166 million and sales of Tandy Brands were $34 million. Thus, both companies were of sufficient size to survive as independent firms, both were profitable and had positive cash flows, and, both firms could also be considered buildable. Tandycrafts owned the profitable and rapidly growing Color Tile subsidiary. Tandy Brands had prospects for significant increases in profitability. In the fiscal year completed just prior to the spin-off, Tandy Brands earned $0.24 per share. But in its first year as a publicly-held company, per share earnings were $1.34. Thus,

Table 6.3

*Sales and Net Income (Loss) of Tandycrafts Subsidiaries
Sold or Spun-Off in 1975 ('000)*

Subsidiaries	Disposition	Revenue	Net Income
Stafford-Lowdon	spun-off	$26,600	$1,053
Decorating and Crafts Magazine	sold	329	28
Royal Tile	sold	570	(44)
Woodie Taylor Vending and Automated and Custom Food Service	sold	2,388	(86)

Source: Annual reports of Tandy Corporation and Tandycrafts, Inc.

both Tandycrafts and Tandy Brands possessed the elements which favored a spin-off rather than a sale.

Following its spin-off from Tandy Corporation, Tandycrafts continued a program of sales and spin-offs using the same criteria as Tandy Corporation had used. In 1975, four firms were sold, and one, Stafford-Lowdon, was spun off (see Table 6.3). Three of the four firms which were sold were small and only one of the four had positive cash flow. Further, Tandycrafts management did not believe that these businesses were buildable. On the other hand, Stafford-Lowdon met at least three of the criteria which favored a spin-off rather than a sale. Sales were relatively large and cash flow was positive. Further, only one or two parties expressed even moderate interest in purchasing the firm. The spin-off of Stafford-Lowdon proved a successful strategy. The stock of Stafford-Lowdon, which was valued at about $8.25 at the time of the spin-off, was acquired by American Standard Inc. in September 1979 for $26.75 per share.

BENEFITS OF SPIN-OFFS

The benefits which Tandycrafts management perceives from spin-offs can be classified into two broad categories—financial and human. Financial considerations included increased appeal of the firm as an investment by the financial community and a more suitable capital structure. Each of these will be discussed, in turn.

The first type of benefit would result from the desire by the financial community for a "pure play," i.e., the opportunity to invest in one business which is considered desirable without having to invest in less desirable businesses at the same time. The concept of the "pure play" is related to what academics call the "clientele effect"—the idea that different stocks appeal to different types of investors. The Tandycrafts/Color Tile spin-off provided considerable evidence for a clientele effect. Following the spin-off, many investors, including at least one mutual fund, who preferred the fast-growing Color Tile to the more steady Tandycrafts, sold stock in the latter and maintained or increased their position in the former. Others sold their Color Tile and kept their Tandycrafts.

While stockholders are obviously concerned with the outcome of the spin-off, on the whole, stockholders are a "silent lot," according to Mr. Michero. But Mr. Michero believed that generally stockholders were pleased to have two pieces of paper rather than one.

Management heard from only two groups of stockholders. The first was made up of arbitrageurs with losses. This group usually charged that their losses were the result of management actions or inactions. But at least for the Tandy Corporation/Tandycrafts spin-offs, their claims were not aggressively pursued. The second group was made up of several stockholders who had great difficulty understanding why Tandycrafts' stock price fell following the spin-off.

The second type of benefit which Tandy management perceived as resulting from spin-offs, relates to various aspects of human resources. The human resource benefits of spin-offs can be classified broadly into benefits resulting from an improved reward structure and benefits resulting from increased managerial efficiency. The benefits of an improved reward structure, in turn, can be categorized into those relating to (1) visibility and mobility and (2) compensation.

Since division level employees of the parent firm prior to the spin-off often become officers of the spun-off firm, their visibility and status are consequently enhanced. Moreover, their performance, which previously could be masked as part of a larger company, stands on its own after the spin-off. Consequently, pressure from stockholders to achieve adequate performance is more direct. Upward mobility of middle management may also be increased.

Mr. Nugent argued that division managers of large firms, who have very lucrative salaries, would be reluctant to leave such jobs to start their own firms, but would often be anxious to head a spun-off division, even at a reduced compensation. On the other hand, some managers naturally will have second thoughts about whether they made the right choice between the parent and spun-off firm. The increased management visibility also is related to the enhanced attractiveness of the firm to the financial community discussed above.

An example of how this increased visibility works is illustrated by the annual reports for Tandy Corporation for the year before (1975) and after (1976) the spin-off of Tandycrafts and Tandy Brands. Tandy Corporation's annual report for fiscal 1975 devotes four pages to a description of the Consumer Electronics Group and two pages each to the Hobby and Handicrafts Group and the Manufacturing and Distribution Group. Most of the companies comprising the latter two groups were spun off. In contrast, Tandy Corporation's 1976 annual report devotes more than eight pages to the firm's consumer electronics business, twice the space which was available prior to the spin-off.

Tandy Corporation management found that some of its businesses required a manager who was a "maintainer" while others required a "builder." These two managerial types were also likely to have different personalities. Difficulties arise in developing a consensus regarding strategic plans and operations when these different types of executives must interface. Further, the development of compensation plans which adequately reward these managers without generating friction is very difficult. Following a spin-off, there is a clearer basis for determining appropriate compensation.

This discussion leads directly to the second human resource benefit of spin-offs—improved managerial performance. This improved performance is believed to result from a more focused managerial attitude. The more focused attitude comes about, in turn, both from simply having fewer businesses to deal with and from the ability to design compensation packages more directly linked with the performance of individual executives.

Georgia-Pacific Corporation: Case Study

Georgia-Pacific Corporation is a major integrated forest products company producing softwood plywood, hardwood plywood, particle board products, and other basic lumber products. The firm also has substantial operations in pulp and paper, gypsum, and chemicals. Georgia-Pacific Corporation was forced to spin-off approximately 18 percent of its total assets in 1973 as a result of a Federal Trade Commission complaint that certain Georgia-Pacific Corporation acquisitions could substantially lessen competition or tend to create a monopoly in the softwood plywood industry. The purpose of this chapter is to describe the impact of this spin-off on the wealth of Georgia-Pacific Corporation's stockholders.

FEDERAL TRADE COMMISSION COMPLAINT

In April 1971, the Federal Trade Commission alleged that during the period 1963-1969 Georgia-Pacific Corporation's acquisition of sixteen companies in the South with 673,000 acres of southern pine trees illegally restrained competition in the softwood plywood industry. The Federal Trade Commission complained that these acquisitions violated the Clayton Act and the Federal Trade Commission Act. To settle the complaint, the Fed-

This case study is adapted from "The Microeconomic Consequences of an Involuntary Corporate Spin-Off," by Ronald J. Kudla and Thomas H. McInish, *Sloan Management Review,* Vol. 22, No. 4, pp. 41-6, by permission of the publisher. Copyright © 1981 by the Sloan Management Review Association. All rights reserved.

eral Trade Commission proposed to formally issue a consent order requiring Georgia-Pacific Corporation to divest itself of the acquired timber lands and eight softwood plywood plants which Georgia-Pacific Corporation had constructed in the South. The proposed order also would have prevented Georgia-Pacific Corporation from acquiring any company in the forest products industry for ten years without prior Federal Trade Commission approval.

Georgia-Pacific Corporation officials disagreed with the Federal Trade Commission complaint, contending that their actions were legal. According to an article in the *Wall Street Journal,* on April 15, 1971, a Georgia-Pacific Corporation spokesman said that Georgia-Pacific Corporation's plywood plants constructed in the South provided new jobs for "literally thousands of people in areas that previously had been depressed" and also produced building materials "vital to critical housing needs." According to the article, the spokesman added that "this action by the Federal Trade Commission is regrettable" and the company will take "all appropriate steps to protect the integrity of the payrolls, plants and timberlands involved."

Although it did not agree with the complaint, Georgia-Pacific Corporation entered into negotiations with the Federal Trade Commission to explore the possibility of a settlement. In December 1972, a settlement was reached. The settlement called for Georgia-Pacific Corporation to form a new corporation, Louisiana-Pacific Corporation, and transfer to it a variety of assets. The assets to be transferred to Louisiana-Pacific Corporation were four softwood plywood plants, two pulpmills, thirty sawmills, and approximately 507,000 acres of timberland in the South and on the West Coast. It was agreed that the net worth of Louisiana-Pacific Corporation would be at least $150 million. As reported in the *Wall Street Journal* on July 25, 1972, the proposed agreement between Georgia-Pacific Corporation and the Federal Trade Commission would also:

—"prohibit the concern from acquiring any interest in any company manufacturing softwood in the United States for ten years.

—"Limit the company's right for five years to acquire or lease pine, mixed pine or hardwood tracts in excess of 25,000 acres unless the lands were to be used for a purpose other than plywood production.

—"Restrict Georgia-Pacific Corporation's acquisition of 10,000 to 25,000 acre tracts of timberland to 100,000 acres annually, if the tracts were to be used for a plywood plant."

Under the agreement, Georgia-Pacific Corporation would be able to purchase up to 100 percent of Louisiana-Pacific Corporation's plywood production in its first operating year and 20 percent less each succeeding year until the fifth year. In the fifth year and thereafter, Georgia-Pacific Corporation would be able to buy 20 percent of Louisiana-Pacific Corporation's plywood.

Key executive changes included Georgia-Pacific Corporation's Vice Chairman and Director, William H. Hunt, becoming Chairman and Chief Executive Officer of Louisiana-Pacific Corporation, and Harry Merlo, Executive Vice President, becoming President and Chief Operating Officer. Lee C. Simpson became a Vice President in charge of Western Sawmill operations, and Donald R. Kayser became Vice President of the Louisiana-Texas division.

The spin-off of Louisiana-Pacific Corporation by Georgia-Pacific Corporation was approved at a special stockholders' meeting on December 8, 1972. Shares in Louisiana-Pacific Corporation were distributed to Georgia-Pacific Corporation stockholders on the basis of one share of Louisiana-Pacific Corporation stock for each four shares of Georgia-Pacific Corporation stock held. The spin-off was completed in January 1973.

VALUATION CONSEQUENCES

Because the spin-off of Louisiana-Pacific Corporation was forced and was not undertaken voluntarily by Georgia-Pacific Corporation, it seems logical to believe that Georgia-Pacific Corporation's management expected the spin-off to lower shareholder wealth. To assess the effects of the spin-off on the wealth of Georgia-Pacific Corporation's shareholders, the residual approach developed by Fama, Fisher, Jensen, and Roll was used.[1] This approach was described in Chapter 5 in the discussion of the Kudla and McInish study of voluntary spin-offs. The residuals represent risk-adjusted abnormal returns which capture the effects of the spin-off on security returns.

Rather than examine the numerical residuals, it is customary to graph the cumulative residuals beginning on an arbitrarily selected date (in this case November 1970). The cumulative residual for any month after the beginning month is the sum of all of the residuals from the beginning month through that given month. The graph of the cumulative residuals from the beginning month has the desirable characteristic that whenever the returns of the stock are greater than expected, the cumulative residual line increases, and whenever the returns of the stock are less than expected, the cumulative residual line decreases. Thus, if the spin-off of Louisiana-Pacific Corporation by Georgia-Pacific Corporation resulted in a decrease in the wealth of Georgia-Pacific Corporation's shareholders relative to the market, the graph of the cumulative residuals is expected to decline and eventually stabilize at a lower level.

The plot of Georgia-Pacific Corporation's cumulative residuals from November 1970 through November 1974 is shown in Figure 7.1. From November 1970 through the month of the complaint, the returns on Georgia-

Pacific Corporation's shares, on a risk-adjusted basis, were lower than expected given the market returns. This result indicates that the Federal Trade Commission complaint was viewed as a negative event and was anticipated as much as eight months prior to its announcement. It is not unusual in studies of this kind for the impact of events to be reflected in stock returns prior to the actual announcement of the event. Statistical tests indicated that the decline in cumulative residuals prior to the spin-off was statistically significant while the postspin-off cumulative residuals were not statistically significant.

The uncertainty surrounding the Federal Trade Commission complaint was resolved with the spin-off of Louisiana-Pacific Corporation at the end of 1972. Thereafter, from February 1973 to March 1974, the shares of Georgia-Pacific Corporation outperformed the market, regaining some of their former losses to the market. After March 1974, the cumulative residuals exhibited the normal random pattern, indicating that the effect of the spin-off had been fully incorporated in the price of Georgia-Pacific Corporation's shares. But the level of cumulative residuals after March 1974 was much lower than in November 1970, indicating that Georgia-Pacific Corporation's shareholders suffered a permanent decrement in wealth after the spin-off.

The pattern of cumulative residuals shown in Figure 7.1 is consistent with market efficiency, where an efficient market is one in which stock prices fully reflect available information so that investors are not able to use that information to earn excess returns (i.e., returns greater than expected given the performance of the market and the risk class of the stock). The residual pattern reflects the arrival of new information to the market concerning the Federal Trade Commission complaint and the likelihood that a forced divestiture would be ordered. Continuous price adjustments occurred as this information was absorbed by the market over time.

RISK EFFECTS

Total risk can be divided into two parts: systematic and unsystematic. Systematic risk is that part of total risk which a security shares with the market as a whole. Hence, systematic risk cannot be diversified away. Unsystematic risk is risk associated with events which affect only a few firms or a single company. Unsystematic risk can be diversified away because in a portfolio unfavorable unsystematic events for one firm are likely to be offset by favorable unsystematic events for another firm. One measure of systematic risk is the beta of the stock as calculated from Sharpe's single index model.[2] Beta measures the degree of sensitivity of a stock's return to market-wide fluctuations. A beta greater than one indicates that a stock is more volatile than the market (and hence more risky than the market), while a beta less than one indicates that a stock is less volatile than the market

Figure 7.1
Georgia-Pacific Corporation's Cumulative Residuals versus Time

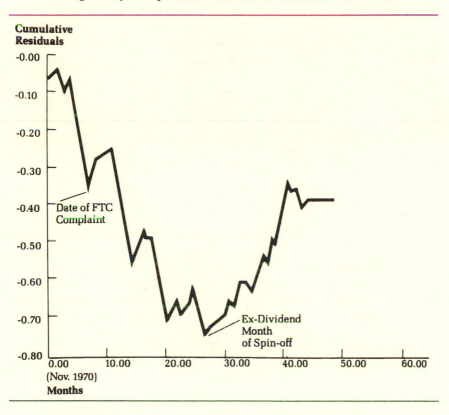

(and hence less risky than the market). The beta of the market is one.

To measure the effect of the spin-off on the systematic risk of Georgia-Pacific Corporation and Louisiana-Pacific Corporation, the before spin-off and after spin-off betas were calculated for Georgia-Pacific Corporation, Louisiana-Pacific Corporation, and its major competitors: Boise-Cascade, Champion International, Evans Products, and Weyerhauser. In addition, a beta was calculated for the portfolio comprising four shares of Georgia-Pacific Corporation and one share of Louisiana-Pacific Corporation. These betas are presented in Table 7.1. Georgia-Pacific Corporation had the largest increase in beta and the only statistically significant increase. One possible explanation of this result is that investors made higher risk

Table 7.1
Before Spin-Off and After Spin-Off Betas

Company (S.I.C.-2400)	Beta		Percent Change	t-value[a]
	Before Spin-off 1968–72 (58 Observations)	After Spin-off 1973–75 (35 Observations)		
Boise-Cascade	1.28	1.53	20%	− .66
Champion International	1.22	1.45	19	− .62
Evans Products	1.68	1.81	8	− .23
Weyerhauser	1.03	.97	− 6	+ .22
G-P	.94[b]	1.75	86	−2.83*
L-P	—	1.63	—	—
G-P and L-P	.94	1.73[c]	83	−2.70*

[a]The t-value is calculated using the following formula:

$$t = \frac{b_1 - b_2}{\sqrt{\left[\frac{(N_1 - 2)(N_1)S_1^2 + (N_2 - 2)(N_2)S_2^2}{N_1 + N_2 - 4}\right]\left[\frac{N_1 + N_2}{N_1 N_2}\right]}},$$

where b_1 = estimated before spin-off beta,

b_2 = estimated after spin-off beta,

N_1 = number of observations before spin-off (58),

N_2 = number of observations after spin-off (35),

S_1 = standard error of b_1,

S_2 = standard error of b_2.

For example, the t-value for G-P is:

$$t_{G-P} = \frac{.936565 - 1.74543}{\sqrt{\left[\frac{(56)(58)(.0378178) + (33)(35)(.0314339)}{35 + 58 - 4}\right]\left[\frac{35 + 58}{35(58)}\right]}},$$

$$= -2.83.$$

See R. L. Winkler and W. L. Hays, *Statistics: Probability, Inference, and Decision* (New York: Holt, Rinehart & Winston, 1975), p. 449.
[b]The beta for G-P for the period January 1967 to the announcement of the FTC complaint in June 1971 was .95.
[c]This beta was calculated using a value-weighted average of the returns on 4 Georgia-Pacific stock shares and 1 Louisiana-Pacific stock share.
*Significant at the .005 level.

Source: Reprinted from ''The Microeconomic Consequences of an Involuntary Corporate Spin-Off,'' by Ronald J. Kudla and Thomas H. McInish, *Sloan Management Review,* Vol. 22, No. 4, p. 43, by permission of the publisher. Copyright © 1981 by The Sloan Management Review Association. All rights reserved.

assessments for Georgia-Pacific Corporation because of the loss of monopoly or market power associated with the spin-off. This is consistent with the charge in the Federal Trade Commission complaint which alleged that the combined firms had monopoly power. The loss of Louisiana-Pacific Corporation's operations, therefore, made future profit and growth prospects of Georgia-Pacific Corporation less certain in the eyes of the investors.

In summary, the spin-off of Louisiana-Pacific Corporation had a negative impact on shareholder wealth as reflected in a decline in the rate of return of Georgia-Pacific Corporation's shares relative to the market return. This loss of shareholder wealth probably resulted from loss of synergies and increased risk. Other factors such as loss of key executives and litigation costs may also have been important. The systematic risk of Georgia-Pacific Corporation's stock as measured by the beta coefficient almost doubled after the spin-off. One possible explanation of this result is that investors viewed Georgia-Pacific Corporation's future earnings and growth prospects as more uncertain because of the loss of market power associated with the spin-off.

NOTES

1. See E. Fama, L. Fisher, M. Jensen, and R. Roll, "The Adjustment of Stock Prices to New Information," *International Economic Review* (February 1969): 1-21.

2. See W. Sharpe, "A Simplified Model for Portfolio Analysis," *Management Science* (January 1963): 277-93.

Gearhart-Owen Industries, Inc.: Case Study

8

Gearhart-Owen Industries, Inc. was founded in 1955 by Marvin Gearhart and Harrold Owen. In May 1978, Gearhart-Owen spun off Pengo Industries, Inc. The details of this spin-off will be described in subsequent sections of this chapter. This chapter is based, in part, on interviews with Marvin Gearhart, Chairman of the Board and President of Gearhart Industries Inc. (formerly Gearhart-Owen Industries, Inc.), Harrold Owen, President and Chairman of the Board of Pengo Industries, Inc., and Wayne Banks, Senior Vice President-Finance and Treasurer of Gearhart Industries, Inc. In addition, much of the information for this case was obtained from the annual reports for Gearhart-Owen and Pengo Industries, and the prospectus for the spin-off (parts of these documents are reproduced here).

For the year-ended January 31, 1978 (just prior to the spin-off), Gearhart-Owen reported sales of $92.0 million, net income of $10.4 million, and assets of $84.3 million. The spun-off businesses constituted about 20 percent of the assets and 12 percent of the earnings of Gearhart-Owen. At the time of the spin-off, Gearhart-Owen shares were traded on the New York Stock Exchange.

Just prior to the spin-off, Gearhart-Owen's principal businesses were (1) performing wireline service operations, (2) manufacturing and selling equipment and supplies which are required to perform wireline service operations, and (3) manufacturing and selling augers and teeth, cable handling equipment, downhole oil tools, explosives, and black powder. Each of these three areas will be discussed in turn.

Figure 8.1
Winch Truck Providing Wireline Services

Reproduced by permission of Gearhart Industries, Inc.

"Wireline services" refers to a variety of services for oil and gas wells. These services are provided using a winch truck (or skid unit) equipped with an armored cable (see Figure 8.1) containing one or more electrical conductors. The cable is used to lower instruments and tools into the well bore. Data concerning specific parameters of the formations penetrated by the well bore are received and recorded by instruments located in the winch. Wireline services are performed at various times (for differing purposes) from the time a well is first drilled until it is depleted and abandoned.

Gearhart-Owen manufactured wireline equipment and supplies at its thirty-one acre site in Forth Worth, Texas, which had approximately 242,000 square feet of manufacturing and office space (an additional building with 65,000 square feet of space was under construction at the time of the spin-off). A substantial portion of these products was used in providing the wireline services described in the previous paragraph. Other major wireline service companies had historically followed the practice of producing wireline service equipment primarily for their own use. Gearhart-Owen was the only major wireline service company that manufactured wireline equipment and supplies for its own use and also marketed its products to the wireline service industry throughout the world. Product sales were made primarily to independent wireline service companies and foreign government agencies.

The third segment of Gearhart-Owen's business was more diverse than the two segments just described. This segment comprised four parts: the Oil Tool Division, the Cable Handling Division, Pengo Corporation, a manufacturer and marketer of augers and teeth, and GOEX, Inc., a manufacturer and marketer of explosives.

The Cable Handling Division was the world's largest producer of cable handling equipment used in electrical power line construction. These cables pull electrical winches into place under highly controlled tension. The equipment was sold both in the United States and overseas. This division was also in the early stages of developing and planning for the manufacture and sale of work-over rigs.

Pengo Corporation manufactured and marketed vertical boring augers, auger teeth, and forged steel teeth used in earth-moving and earth-boring machines (including trenching machines, back-hoes, and power shovels), on electric power lines, and in a variety of other construction projects. The products were manufactured in its own forging plant. Pengo Corporation was the largest manufacturer of vertical boring augers in the United States.

GOEX, Inc. manufactured and sold explosives and black powder and performed the service of loading explosive charges for commercial customers. The black powder plant, which produced fuse, blasting, propellant, sporting, and fireworks grades of black powder, was the only such plant operating in the United States.

REASON FOR THE SPIN-OFF

The reason for the spin-off of Pengo by Gearhart-Owen is easy to determine—significant differences between the two founders, Mr. Gearhart and Mr. Owen. The cause of these differences is not so easy to identify and, indeed, may not be clearly understood even by the parties involved. The stated reason for the spin-off was differing perspectives regarding the operations of the business. But a much more serious motivating factor was the disintegration of the trust and goodwill between the founders. Misunderstanding followed misunderstanding so that by the time of the spin-off, the management was unable to function as a team. Hence, it is difficult to separate the business and personality motives for the spin-off. In order to aid in an understanding of the spin-off, the president's letter to the stockholders in the 1978 annual report of Gearhart-Owen and the 1978 annual report of Pengo, as well as parts of the prospectus are provided here (see Figures 8.2, 8.3, 8.4).

According to the prospectus covering the spin-off (see Figure 8.2), the key reason for the spin-off was the development over the years of differing perspectives as to the future course of the business. Mr. Gearhart believed that Gearhart-Owen should concentrate exclusively on its wireline business. According to Mr. Gearhart, the wireline business was the most profitable of Gearhart-Owen's businesses and, thus, represented the best use of Gearhart-Owen's funds. In his letter to the shareholders (see Figure 8.3), Mr. Gearhart emphasizes that even though the wireline logging industry is 50 years old "this business is growing faster than any other time since its inception."

On the other hand, Mr. Owen believed that Gearhart-Owen should use some of its resources to acquire and operate nonwireline-related businesses. Mr. Owen believed that there were sufficient funds to expand both wireline and nonwireline businesses. This emphasis is especially evident in the next to the last paragraph of Mr. Owen's first letter to Pengo stockholders following the spin-off (see Figure 8.4).

The difference between Mr. Gearhart and Mr. Owen developed over a four- to five-year period preceding the spin-off. In 1976, there had been some discussion of a separation and spin-off of the service and nonservice businesses of Gearhart-Owen, but at the time there was insufficient support due to the hope that differences between Mr. Gearhart and Mr. Owen could be resolved. But by 1977, the situation had deteriorated to the point where the firm's investment bankers proposed the spin-off that was subsequently approved.

The most significant factor precipitating the spin-off was the deterioration in the relationship between Mr. Gearhart and Mr. Owen. By the time of the spin-off, the two founders of Gearhart-Owen hardly talked to each other and had even ceased sharing the same secretary. Other executives were paralyzed because they reported to two bosses with differing views.

Figure 8.2

Excerpts from Pengo Industries Prospectus

PROSPECTUS SUMMARY

The following is a summary of certain information contained in the body of this Prospectus and is qualified in its entirety by the detailed information and the financial statements appearing elsewhere herein.

Reasons for Spin-Off

The majority of GOI's business operations consists of wireline services (for a description of "wireline services," see INTRODUCTORY STATEMENT on page 6). In connection with such services, GOI manufactures and sells certain equipment and supplies, which are required to perform wireline service operations. Such business operations are herein referred to as GOI's "Wireline Business."

The remainder of GOI's business operations is non-wireline-related and consists of the manufacture and sale of augers and teeth, cable handling equipment, downhole oil tools, and explosives. These business operations (excepting only certain dual-purpose equipment — See BUSINESS on page 14) are herein referred to as GOI's "Non-Wireline Business." See BUSINESS on page 14.

The board of directors of GOI, after extensive review, concluded that it would be in the best interests of GOI and its shareholders to transfer the properties comprising GOI's Non-Wireline Business to Pengo. GOI's two key officers (and founders), Mr. Marvin Gearhart and Mr. Harrold D. Owen, have developed over the years differing perspectives regarding GOI's Non-Wireline Business. Foremost among these differences is the opinion of Mr. Gearhart that GOI should concentrate on, and limit the scope of its business operations to, its Wireline Business, whereas Mr. Owen's opinion is that GOI should use some of its resources to acquire and operate businesses which are not wireline-related. As a result of these differing perspectives, there has not been a unanimity of opinion at the top management level of GOI as to the emphasis that should be placed on the Non-Wireline Business and the resources, time, and effort of GOI which should be devoted thereto.

Because of the diverse nature of GOI's Wireline and Non-Wireline businesses, and, because of differing management opinions as to the emphasis to be given to each of these businesses, the board of directors of GOI decided on the spin-off arrangement as a logical resolution of the situation. Mr. Gearhart is the president and chief executive officer of GOI, which has retained and is operating the Wireline Business, and Mr. Owen is the president and chief executive officer of Pengo, which has obtained and is operating the Non-Wireline Business.

GOI's board of directors believes that the spin-off transaction described above will result in more intensive and specialized management of each of the two different businesses and that the operational and financial progress of the two businesses, each with a distinct business direction, will be more visible to shareholders and will provide a stimulus for each executive to maintain an even higher degree of management excellence.

On November 1, 1977, GOI transferred the properties comprising its Non-Wireline Business to Pengo in exchange for all of Pengo's presently issued and outstanding shares of common stock (1,463,895 shares) and the agreement by Pengo to assume certain of GOI's liabilities, including indebtedness in the amount of $5,400,000 and certain other contingent liabilities. See PENGO INDUSTRIES, INC.— PRO FORMA CAPITALIZATION on page 8 and LEGAL PROCEEDINGS on page 23. Since the basis of the distribution is one Pengo share for every two GOI shares held, and since the number of shares of GOI's issued and outstanding common stock has increased since November 1, 1977, and might increase to a maximum of 3,220,175 shares prior to the record date referred to below, Pengo has also agreed to deliver to GOI within ten days after such record date, a certificate for that number of additional shares of Pengo common stock necessary to effect the spin-off equal to one-half of GOI's common stock issued and outstanding as of the record date. GOI is spinning-off Pengo by distributing Pengo's common stock to GOI shareholders on a pro-rata basis.

Figure 8.2 *(continued)*

Certificates for the shares of common stock of Pengo are being distributed on or about June 20, 1978, to GOI shareholders of record on June 9, 1978, on the basis of one share of Pengo stock for every two shares of GOI stock held. No fractional shares are being issued but, in lieu thereof, the First National Bank of Fort Worth, Fort Worth, Texas, as agent, will sell for GOI shareholders entitled to fractional interests, the shares representing the sum of the fractional share interests which would otherwise have been issued. The net proceeds of such sale will be paid over ratably to the GOI shareholders entitled thereto. If a market for Pengo's shares does not develop, the sale of such fractional interests may be adversely effected. See SPIN-OFF AND DISTRIBUTION OF SHARES on page 6.

Federal Income Taxes

GOI has received rulings from the Internal Revenue Service to the effect that the spin-off will not result in taxable gain or loss to GOI or to the GOI shareholders (except for cash received by GOI shareholders in lieu of fractional shares) and that the basis of the GOI common stock owned by each GOI shareholder is to be allocated between such GOI shares and the shares of common stock of Pengo received in the distribution, in proportion to their respective fair market values on the date of distribution. See FEDERAL INCOME TAXES on page 7.

Market for Shares of Pengo

Prior to the date hereof there has been no trading market for the common stock of Pengo. An application for the listing of Pengo's common stock on the New York Stock Exchange has been approved. See SPIN-OFF AND DISTRIBUTION OF SHARES on page 6.

Ex-Dividend Trading in GOI Stock

The record date for determining the shareholders of GOI entitled to receive the Pengo stock is June 9, 1978. The date on which the Pengo stock is distributable to the GOI shareholders is on or about June 20, 1978. It is expected that GOI common stock will commence trading ex-dividend on the New York Stock Exchange on June 5, 1978. See SPIN-OFF AND DISTRIBUTION OF SHARES on page 6.

Dividend Policy

Pengo has concluded that, initially, dividends will not be paid on the common stock; any earnings will be retained for expansion and for increased working capital. See DESCRIPTION OF COMMON STOCK — DIVIDEND POLICY on page 23.

Pengo Industries, Inc.

Pengo was incorporated on October 3, 1977, as a Texas corporation, in order to acquire from GOI the properties comprising its Non-Wireline Business. Pengo's principal office is in the Everman National Bank Building, 1000 Everman Road, Fort Worth, Texas (mailing address: P. O. Box 40530, Fort Worth, Texas 76140), and its telephone number at that office is 817-293-7110. See PENGO INDUSTRIES, INC. — ORGANIZATION on page 8.

Extract from the 1978 Pengo Industries Prospectus, pp. 3-4.

Figure 8.3
Letter to Shareholders

The electrical wireline logging business is now 50 years old and today this business is growing faster than at any other time since its inception. As oil and gas become harder to find and as producers endeavor to extract a larger percent of these products from the underground formations, electrical wireline logging becomes even more important.

Our company is fortunate to be situated in such a dynamic, growing industry and we are even more fortunate that once again we can report that we not only kept abreast of market growth, but were also able to achieve a greater share of the market, which is equally significant. Wireline-related revenues (which will be our company's continuing operations) increased from $53.5 million in fiscal year 1977 to $76.2 million in fiscal year 1978.

The internal reorganization of the company into wireline-related activities (to be retained) and non-wireline-related activities (to be spun off) has been completed and the legal separation of the two entities can be expected to occur reasonably soon. This will result in Gearhart-Owen being a pure wireline service and products company and management can concentrate on the problems of refining and expanding our expertise in this area. As a result of this new singleness of purpose and concentrated dedication of effort, we expect to gain even more market share in this rapidly-growing market.

The industry has a major technological transition on its hands brought about by the application of minicomputers to logging operations. The advancing technology of the electronics and computer industries continues to be almost mind-boggling and our industry faces a real challenge to utilize these new technological developments. Although we believe we have a lead in the industry with our DDL* (Direct Digital Logging) system, we already are working on even more advanced systems. Our company is fortunate to be positioned so that we can take advantage of the new technology. That is to say, we are not confronted with the constraint of obsoleting our entire fleet in order to utilize the new technology and yet we do have a sizeable base on which to build. It is as important to have a strong organization for applying technology as it is to have the technology.

Our organization has been built over a period of years and it is one of the main strengths of our company. Several times a year we finish projects and put new tools and systems into service that have only been a few months in development. In most instances, these products out-perform competitors' products that required years to develop. This has built confidence in our people and they readily accept new challenges for even more difficult assignments. Again, it is the combination of new technology and the competence of our organization that makes our progress so exciting.

We are often asked how we can compete with the larger companies. Part of the answer is that 70 percent of our manufacturing output is sold to outside customers, thereby spreading development costs over a volume of business that is much larger than that of our own fleet of service units. But perhaps more importantly, we honestly believe a smaller organization has efficiencies not found in larger conglomerate structures.

There is much more to an effective organization than its technical strength. During recent months we have set up a data base system to provide better information for all operations within the company. Such information will greatly assist long-range planning and will help provide the controls necessary for implementation of management's plans.

Significant capital expenditures are being made to increase production capacity and provide for the expected growth of the company without inhibiting our plans to continue increasing the cash dividend.

We look forward to taking full advantage of the tremendous growth opportunities ahead and hope all of our shareholders and employees share with management the satisfaction of making a contribution to our industry, while setting new sales and earnings records for our company.

Marvin Gearhart

MARVIN GEARHART
Chairman of the Board and President

*Trademark of Gearhart-Owen Industries, Inc.

Extract from the 1978 Annual Report of Gearhart-Owen Industries, Inc., pp. 2-3.

Figure 8.4
To Our Shareholders

To Our Shareholders:

I would like to welcome each of you as a stockholder in Pengo Industries, Inc. This is our first annual report since our spinoff from Gearhart-Owen Industries, Inc. (GOI). The period since our spinoff has been spent in numerous activities. The spinoff of a company of our size has been an enormous operation that has been accompanied by numerous problems, some of which have been resolved and some for which we are still in the process of arriving at solutions that are totally satisfactory. In this letter we would like to make you aware of the tremendous potential that we see for the Company, while at the same time not neglecting to point out the problems.

We have spent considerable time and money during the past year in overcoming some of the initial handicaps we faced. We have built a new plant and machine shop facility, greatly improved our accounting department and data processing system, and resolved major problems in our oil tool inventory. In addition to these problem solving efforts, we have also begun our new Well Servicing Division, strengthened our program of marketing and product development for our existing lines of business, and planned for future capital needs of all our operations.

The lines of business assumed in the spinoff should, on their own, make Pengo a company of average profitability. I believe, however, our shareholders and employees are expecting Pengo to be more than that. To that goal we have developed an ambitious plan to enter the well workover business with a well servicing rig designed by Pengo, which will be capable of performing almost all the services required to complete a well once it is drilled, to recomplete a well in a new zone, or to workover a producing zone.

The new rig utilizes a substantially different concept. It is hydraulically powered rather than mechanically drawn. Other than being hydraulically powered, the rig does not appear any different from a conventional workover rig, and will not be able to perform any service that other workover companies could not offer should they elect to do so.

The reason we believe the Pengo rig has a great potential is that since it is powered by hydraulics, we can reduce weight on the conventional parts of the rig used to pull the tubing from the well and put this weight into equipment such as high pressure pumps and a hoist system to provide logging, perforating and other wireline services.

This wireline capability and the hydraulic power concept will enable the Pengo rig to perform, with the single unit, services presently requiring a number of different service companies' units, equipment and personnel.

Pengo intends to concentrate on a line of electro-mechanical tools which can be used in concert with

Figure 8.4 *(continued)*
To Our Shareholders

the tubing and pumps to provide a combination of services which will be unique and more economical to the oil operator.

We are not so naive as to believe that the Pengo plan cannot and will not be emulated by others, but we do believe Pengo has a rather unique talent and opportunity to be the leader from a technical standpoint.

The prototype rig was first tested outside the shop on December 18 and will be placed in the field for testing about January 1. It will continue to be used to test certain concepts which will be placed on the subsequent rigs. The rig as shown on the inside cover has a derrick and drawworks mounted on a self propelled carrier. The derrick is approximately 100 feet tall in the extended position and is believed to be capable of pulling 200,000 pounds.

We have been able to place orders for the carriers (engine and wheels) with deliveries of two per month beginning in late April or early May. The derrick, drawworks and pumps will be built during January, February and March so that the rigs can be rapidly assembled when the carriers are delivered.

In order to expedite Pengo's entry into the well workover business, we plan to acquire several small workover companies and convert some of their conventional rigs to provide wireline service. Later, the conventional rigs could be replaced with the Pengo hydraulic rig.

Even though we expect that it will be late in fiscal 1979 before we begin to see any meaningful contributions to our earnings as a result of these new rigs, we believe future years will prove the wisdom of embarking on this new line of business.

We are also devoting substantial engineering effort and are spending significant funds to develop new tools for our Oil Tool Division. By doing so, we plan to increase its market share from the presently estimated level of about 5%. Since only a portion of the product line of the Oil Tool Division, as it was structured under GOI, was spunoff, we have encountered some unusual

problems which are not yet completely resolved. Two of the most significant problems were an oversupply of certain finished goods in inventory and no production facilities or equipment to produce the tools.

In addition, two of the most profitable lines of this division, setting tools and bridge plugs, were retained by GOI, and Pengo is prohibited from selling or leasing these in the U.S. until November 1980.

We have written off or sold for scrap value over $800,000 of the finished goods inventory, which accounts for the major portion of the loss sustained by this division. The inventory still remains high because it contains a disproportionate share of slow moving products, but we believe no further inventory adjustments will be necessary. The other primary factor relating to the overall loss of this division is that our service revenue of approximately $600,000 was not enough to support the $2,000,000 of selling and administrative expenses associated with it. The marketing structure had been built for a service organization, but during the eight months ended September 30, 1978, only 17% of the revenues were from service work. It is our opinion that if we can reach at least a 35% level of service revenues and sustain our present level of tool sales, then this division would become profitable. (Please refer to Management's Discussion and Analysis" on page eleven for additional information.)

To overcome these adverse factors, we have taken the following steps. In October we moved into our new manufacturing facility and have almost completed installation of machines which have the capacity to produce about 60% of the required oil tools. An increased engineering staff has broadened the product line, we have increased prices, and instituted an incentive system for the oil tool sales and service personnel. A plan is underway to integrate the Oil Tool Division with Pengo Well Services to share the cost of distributing the oil tool line of products through utilization of common field facilities.

All of our other lines of business are concentrating on improving market share, productivity and efficiency. Many of our businesses are enjoying increasing international marketing opportunities, and we anticipate overseas revenue to increase substantially from the present level of about 15%.

Our heavy capital expenditure requirements have extended our debt/equity ratio to a higher level than we would like, particularly with the recent rapid increase in interest rates. We believe, however, that it is to the best interests of the shareholders to keep this level of leverage at the present time and that Pengo is in a good financial posture. Pengo's established businesses have good facilities and equipment and no significant capital expenditures are planned for them for fiscal 1979.

In August, Pengo acquired General Texas Corporation (GTC) for $20,000 of Pengo stock. In connection with this acquisition, Pengo will retire $543,000 of GTC's debt with stock in early 1979. GTC has several chemical products in the automotive market and has in process about $3,500,000 of government manufacturing and processing contracts.

In fiscal 1979 we plan to continue with our development, expansion and acquisition plans in the well servicing area. We also plan to continue with the development of the oil tool division. Management believes that this division, while plagued by numerous initial problems, has great potential. Finally, we plan to expand our market share in those lines of business that are already contributing significantly to the profit of the company and we believe Pengo's long-range prospects are good.

For the Board of Directors and Management,
Sincerely,

Harrold D. Owen

Harrold D. Owen
President and Chairman of the Board
Fort Worth, Texas

December 22, 1978

Extract from the 1978 Pengo Industries, Inc. Annual Report, pp. 2-3.

ASSESSMENT OF THE SPIN-OFF

As surprising as it may seem in light of the foregoing discussion of the reasons for the spin-off, Gearhart-Owen and Pengo management are in agreement on their assessment of the spin-off (though for differing reasons). Both managements believe that a spin-off is not the best alternative for solving management differences. Mr. Gearhart believes that Gearhart-Owen would have been better off if Mr. Owen had left through resignation rather than as a result of the spin-off. Mr. Owen believes that personally he may have been better off to have left Gearhart-Owen and formed his own firm rather than having become head of the spun-off firm.

The reason for Mr. Gearhart's view was that the spin-off immediately created a competitor for Gearhart-Owen. Mr. Owen's view was based on his belief that the spin-off was unfair. Reasons for differing perspectives on the fairness of the spin-off are discussed below.

DETAILS OF THE SPIN-OFF

Immediately following the decision to establish two companies through a spin-off, plans began to be made to implement the decision. Details were negotiated between Mr. Owen, various attorneys, and officials of Gearhart-Owen. Due to the deteriorated relationships among Gearhart-Owen officials, the negotiation process was more adversarial than cooperative.

The vehicle to be spun-off, Pengo Industries, Inc., was incorporated on October 3, 1977. On November 1, Pengo Corporation, GOEX, Inc., and Gearhart-Owen's cable handling and oil tool divisions were transferred to Pengo Industries in exchange for Pengo Industries common stock. Two of the most profitable product lines of the Oil Tool Division, setting tools and bridge plugs, were retained by Gearhart-Owen. Gearhart-Owen retained assets which had been used in these transferred businesses, but which had also been used in its other businesses. No production facilities or equipment for the manufacturing operations of the cable handling or oil tool divisions were transferred to Pengo. Instead, Pengo purchased land and constructed new facilities. Pengo rented space from Gearhart-Owen until it could complete its new facilities.

Table 8.1 shows the revenues and operating income of Gearhart-Owen for the five fiscal years immediately preceding the spin-off. The results for wireline-related and other businesses are shown separately. Both the wireline-related and other businesses grew rapidly, with the wireline-related segment experiencing the most rapid growth. In the fiscal year preceding the spin-off, the revenues of Pengo constituted 20.4 percent of the sales of Gearhart-Owen (including those of Pengo), but Pengo's earnings constituted only 12.0 percent of the earnings of Gearhart-Owen. Although not apparent from the financial statements, the auger and teeth business trans-

Table 8.1
Information as to Lines of Business

	YEAR ENDED JANUARY 31 – IN THOUSANDS OF DOLLARS				
	1978	1977	1976	1975	1974
Revenues					
Wireline-related .... $	76,186	$ 53,496	$ 44,410	$ 32,060	$ 19,957
Other	18,835	16,727	18,572	15,477	11,085
Less Inter-Group Revenue .. (	3,025)	(1,200)	(616)	(315)	(119)
Net Revenue .... $	91,996	$ 69,023	$ 62,366	$ 47,222	$ 30,923
Operating Income					
Wireline-related .... $	19,020	$ 11,670	$ 10,277	$ 7,235	$ 3,265
Other	2,295	3,091	3,191	2,041	1,054
Less Corporate Expenses ... (	2,230)	(1,720)	(1,438)	(1,439)	(935)
Income Before Taxes .... $	19,085	$ 13,041	$ 12,030	$ 7,837	$ 3,384

Source: 1978 Annual Report of Gearhart-Owen Industries, Inc., p. 9.

ferred to Pengo Industries had constituted among the most profitable business of Gearhart-Owen. A more detailed income statement for Pengo for
the year ended January 31, 1978, and the eight months ended September
30, 1978, is provided in Table 8.2.

As of January 31, 1978, the assets of Gearhart-Owen totaled $84.3 mil-
lion; of these $17.5 million (20.8 percent) were transferred to Pengo. Table
8.3 (taken from the Pengo 1978 annual report) provides balance sheets for
Pengo as of January 31, 1978, and September 30, 1978. As of January 31,
1978, the assets of Pengo comprised $12.0 million of current assets, $5.2
million of property, plant and equipment, and $0.3 million of other assets.
These assets were matched by debt and equity as follows: current liabilities,
$3.1 million; long-term debt, $5.7 million; other liabilities, $0.2 million;
and equity, $8.5 million. The long-term debt represented primarily bank
lines taken over from Gearhart-Owen. As of the January 31, 1978, balance
sheet, Pengo's equity constituted 48 percent of its capitalization; this percentage closely matched the capital structure of Gearhart-Owen, which had
49.6 percent of its assets as equity. But the September 30, 1978, balance
sheet indicates a different situation. While equity was essentially unchanged,
assets had grown to $23.2 million. As a result, equity had declined to only
about 36 percent of total assets.

The differences between the January 31, 1978, balance sheet and the September 30, 1978, balance sheet indicate the basis of the disagreement between Pengo management and Gearhart-Owen management as to the fairness of the spin-off. Based on the January statement, Gearhart-Owen
management believes that since Pengo's equity constituted the same per-

centage of total assets as that of Pengo, the asset/liability transfers were fair. On the other hand, Pengo management believes that the September statement indicates a truer (and less favorable) picture of Pengo's position at the time of the spin-off. Perhaps a closer look at the differences between the current assets and property, plant and equipment accounts for the two statements will help illuminate the differing perspectives.

First, between January 31 and September 30, current assets grew from $12.0 million to $14.2 million, largely as a result of increased inventories (see Table 8.4). This inventory growth took place despite the fact that Pengo found it necessary to write off $600,000 in connection with inventories sold for scrap. Pengo views its inventories at the time of the spin-off as overstated by that amount. On the other hand, Gearhart-Owen's management contends that these inventories were properly associated with Pengo, especially considering that the inventories were accumulated by Pengo's management while they were employees of Gearhart-Owen. Moreover, according to Gearhart-Owen management, these inventories were conservatively valued under all contingencies except that they were scrap.

Table 8.2
Consolidated Statements of Operations

Consolidated Statements of Operations

	Eight Months Ended September 30, 1978	Year Ended January 31, 1978
		(NOTE 2)
Net Revenues	$ 14,145,000	$ 18,835,000
Costs and Expenses:		
Cost of manufacturing (Note 3)	9,928,000	12,313,000
Selling, general and administrative expenses	3,828,000	4,243,000
Interest expense	441,000	418,000
	14,197,000	16,974,000
Income (Loss) Before Taxes	(52,000)	1,861,000
Provision for Income Taxes (Note 6)	30,000	950,000
Net Income (Loss)	$(82,000)	$ 911,000
Weighted Average Common Shares Outstanding	1,535,628	1,535,337
Net (Loss) Per Share	$ (.05)	$ —
Pro Forma Net Income Per Share (Note 2)	$ —	$ .59

The accompanying notes are an integral part of these statements.

Source: 1978 Pengo Industries, Inc. Annual Report, p. 12.

Table 8.3
Consolidated Balance Sheets

Consolidated Balance Sheets

Assets	September 30, 1978	January 31, 1978 (NOTE 2)
Current Assets		
Cash	$ 617,000	$ 905,000
Refundable Federal income taxes (Note 6)	436,000	—
Accounts receivable trade, net of allowance for doubtful accounts of $204,000 and $148,000	3,738,000	2,877,000
Inventories, at lower of cost or market (Note 3)	8,893,000	7,975,000
Prepaid and other	506,000	196,000
Total current assets	14,190,000	11,953,000
Property, plant and equipment at cost (Notes 5 and 10)		
Land	1,142,000	752,000
Plant and equipment, net of accumulated depreciation of $2,637,000 and $2,257,000	7,191,000	4,489,000
	8,333,000	5,241,000
Other Assets	660,000	323,000
	$ 23,183,000	$ 17,517,000
Liabilities and Stockholders' Equity		
Current Liabilities		
Accounts payable	$ 1,923,000	$ 1,951,000
Accrued expenses	1,027,000	910,000
Accrued income taxes	63,000	145,000
Current maturities of long-term debt (Note 5)	463,000	71,000
Total current liabilities	3,476,000	3,077,000
Long-Term Debt, net of current maturities (Note 5)	10,943,000	5,718,000
Other Liabilities	325,000	221,000
Commitments and Contingent Liabilities (Note 11)		
Stockholders' Equity (Notes 2, 4, 5, 7, and 13):		
Common stock, $.25 par value, 7,000,000 shares authorized, 1,537,663 and 1,535,337 issued and outstanding	384,000	384,000
Capital surplus	2,285,000	2,265,000
Retained earnings	5,770,000	5,852,000
	8,439,000	8,501,000
	$ 23,183,000	$ 17,517,000

The accompanying notes are an integral part of these statements.

Source: 1978 Pengo Industries, Inc. Annual Report, p. 13.

Table 8.4

Note 3. Inventories

Note 3. Inventories

The opening and closing inventories used in the
computation of cost of manufacturing are as follows:

	January 31, 1977	January 31, 1978	September 30, 1978
Raw materials	$1,909,000	$1,887,000	$2,715,000
Work in progress	1,170,000	711,000	1,062,000
Finished goods	3,382,000	5,377,000	5,116,000
	$6,461,000	$7,975,000	$ 8,893,000

During the period ended September 30, 1978, the
Company sold certain inventory in which it had an
oversupply resulting in a charge to cost of manufacturing
of approximately $600,000 in excess of the sale price.

Source: 1978 Pengo Industries Inc. Annual Report, p. 16.

Next, property, plant, and equipment increased by $3.4 million from Jan-
uary to September (see Table 8.5). The increased investment in land and
buildings largely represented the expenditure of $1.4 million for nine acres
and a 86,000 square foot facility in Fort Worth. From Pengo's viewpoint,
these expenditures were necessary to replace the production facilities and
executive offices retained by Gearhart-Owen. Recall that Gearhart-Owen
had a 242,000 square foot building. But from Gearhart-Owen's perspective,
these expenditures were larger than necessary. For example, at the time of
the spin-off, Pengo occupied only 25,000 square feet of Gearhart-Owen's
manufacturing facilities.

Another way to look at the issue of the fairness of the asset/liability
transfers is in terms of profitability of Pengo in relationship to the assets
assumed. While Pengo received about 20 percent of Gearhart-Owen's assets
and liabilities, these assets produced only 12 percent of Gearhart-Owen's
earnings. Hence, from Pengo's viewpoint the liabilities it assumed were
excessive when compared with its ability to service these liabilities. But from
Gearhart-Owen's point of view, the lack of profitability of certain of the
spun-off lines of business was exactly the reason for not wanting to continue to invest in these lines. Also, recall that the tooth and auger business
was very profitable.

Several additional details in connection with the spin-off which may be of interest should be mentioned. In connection with the reorganization, Gearhart-Owen and Pengo entered into an agreement not to compete with each other in the territorial United States for a period of three years from the date of the spin-off. The agreement covered those lines of business in which each respective company was engaged at the time of the spin-off.

The spin-off of Pengo was accomplished by the distribution of one Pengo share for every two shares of Gearhart-Owen held as of June 9, 1978. As mentioned above, at the time of the spin-off, the shares of Gearhart-Owen were listed on the New York Stock Exchange. Prior to the distribution, Pengo shares were approved for listing on the New York Stock Exchange.

Of course, following the spin-off, Pengo faced the necessity of creating entirely new accounting, personnel, and similar systems. Other than unusual expenses, the development of these systems posed no abnormal difficulties.

A favorable Internal Revenue Service ruling that the spin-off was nontaxable was considered essential to the spin-off plan. Most of the stockholders of Gearhart-Owen had a very low basis in their shares. If the distribution of the Pengo stock had been considered a dividend taxable as ordinary income, Mr. Gearhart, Mr. Owen, and many other stockholders would have been required to pay taxes of up to 70 percent of the value of the shares distributed.

Table 8.5
Note 10. Property, Plant and Equipment

Note 10. Property, Plant and Equipment

Property, plant and equipment as reflected on the accompanying consolidated balance sheet is comprised of the following classifications:

	September 30, 1978	January 31, 1978
Land	$ 1,142,000	$ 752,000
Buildings and improvements	3,054,000	1,685,000
Machinery and equipment	6,184,000	4,296,000
Rental equipment	590,000	765,000
	$10,970,000	$ 7,498,000

Source: 1978 Pengo Industries, Inc. Annual Report, p. 18.

Besides the very large tax liability, actual payment of the taxes may have resulted in the necessity to raise funds by selling large blocks of Pengo or Gearhart-Owen stock. Based on the relative values of the shares of Gearhart-Owen and Pengo following the spin-off, stockholders' basis was allocated 94.2253 percent to Gearhart-Owen and 5.7747 percent to Pengo.

This chapter described the 1978 spin-off of Pengo Industries from Gearhart-Owen Industries, Inc., a spin-off which resulted from disagreements among the company's two founders concerning investment policies. These disagreements ultimately led to an inability of top management to work together to achieve corporate objectives. As a result of the spin-off, two separate companies were formed, each headed by one of the two founders of Gearhart-Owen Industries. Thus, the spin-off accomplished its objective of establishing a better managerial environment. Nevertheless, in retrospect, the managements of Gearhart-Owen and Pengo believe that other approaches (such as resignations) may have been more suitable for restoring management harmony.

The Santa Anita Companies: Case Study

9

This chapter describes the merger of Santa Anita Consolidated, Inc. (Santa Anita) into Santa Anita Realty Enterprises, Inc. (Realty), and the distribution to Realty's shareholders of common stock in a wholly-owned subsidiary, Santa Anita Operating Company (Operating Company). The reason for the merger and subsequent spin-off of Operating Company was to enable Realty to conduct its business as a real estate investment trust (REIT). The primary benefit of the REIT form of organization is to reduce Santa Anita's federal income tax and, consequently, increase the amounts of Santa Anita's income available for distribution to its shareholders as dividends. This benefit is due to the fact that REITs may deduct dividends paid to shareholders from income before computing their federal income tax. For other types of corporations, dividends are payable only after payment of corporate income taxes.

This chapter is divided into three sections. The first section gives a historical perspective on the businesses of Santa Anita Consolidated, Inc., including a discussion of corporate objectives and policies. The second section describes the plan of reorganization including its purpose, the parties involved, and the factors that were considered in arriving at the final decision to undertake a spin-off. The last section covers the details of the federal tax consequences of the reorganization.

BACKGROUND (PRIOR TO REORGANIZATION)

The principal businesses of Santa Anita Consolidated, Inc. were thoroughbred horse racing, commercial real estate development, and shopping center investments. Thoroughbred horse racing was conducted primarily through Los Angeles Turf Club, Inc., a wholly-owned subsidiary. Los Angeles Turf Club operated Santa Anita Park (which was owned by Santa Anita). The Los Angeles Turf Club conducts a 78-day meet at Santa Anita Park each year. In addition, The Oak Tree Racing Association conducted its 24-day racing meet at Santa Anita Park through a leasing arrangement with Santa Anita. This meet, coupled with the 78-day meet of the Los Angeles Turf Club, gave Santa Anita Park an effective utilization of 102 days per year.

Santa Anita's horse racing operations had achieved steady growth during the 1970s by emphasizing (1) an award-winning advertising campaign, (2) continued expansion of marketing promotions to develop new fans for racing, (3) expanded media coverage, and (4) attraction of the best jockeys and top horses from all over the United States. The marketing and promotion effort relied heavily on the direct mail approach. By analyzing the characteristics of individuals who had attended Santa Anita Park over the years, management was able to direct promotional programs at specific demographic groupings. Emphasis was also given to handling groups ranging in size from 25 to 500 persons. The use of frequent specialty promotions on racing days such as Calendar Day, Cap Day, and Jacket Day further built attendance levels.

The commercial development business of Santa Anita was conducted primarily by Santa Anita Development Corporation, a wholly-owned subsidiary of Santa Anita. Santa Anita Development was the West's largest developer of neighborhood convenience shopping centers. In the beginning of fiscal 1978, Santa Anita Development changed its operating philosophy from one of developing properties exclusively for sale to investors to one of developing some properties for sale and retaining others for investment. Under this approach, the sale of real estate would provide cash for continuing operations and create a respectable level of earnings. The retention of properties for investment was expected to increase Santa Anita Development's real net worth substantially, through appreciation and rental income on the retained properties. As the market value of these properties increased over time, Santa Anita Development could expect to earn a significant return from appreciation when these properties were sold.

Consistent with this new philosophy, in fiscal 1978 Santa Anita Development set aside as investments six properties having aggregate equities of about $1.7 million. It was estimated that these properties when completed and fully leased would generate net cash flow after debt service of approximately $160,000. During fiscal 1979, Santa Anita Development continued to set aside projects for their investment portfolio. By June 30, 1979, nineteen projects with a cost of $14 million were in the portfolio. Net cash flow after debt service for these projects was in excess of $700,000. While the change in Santa Anita Development's operating philosophy proved fortuitous in light of the subsequent decision to form a REIT, this was not a factor at the time the change in operating philosophy was made. A number of the properties accumulated following the change in philosophy would be contributed to the REIT at the time of its formation.

The third business operated by Santa Anita comprised shopping center investments. Santa Anita's primary shopping center investment was a 50 percent equity interest in Santa Anita Fashion Park, a one million square foot major regional shopping center located on a corner of Santa Anita's property in Arcadia, California. In addition, Santa Anita received annual ground rental payments of $477,000 for its ownership of the 73 acres underlying the Fashion Park.

The revenues and operating profits from 1974 through 1979 for Santa Anita's lines of business are shown in Table 9.1. As shown in Table 9.1, revenues from Santa Anita's principal businesses, thoroughbred racing, and

Table 9.1

Santa Anita's Revenues and Operating Profits by Industry Segment, 1974-1979

Revenues ($Millions)	1979	1978	1977	1976	1975	1974	Compound Annual Rate of Growth %
Thoroughbred Racing	$40.3	37.2	32.7	30.3	26.9	24.3	10.7%
Commercial Development	23.4	30.0	22.5	15.0	16.4	13.5	11.6
Real Estate Investments[1]	1.2	.9	.9	.7	.4	—	31.6
Other[2]	.8	.3	.5	.9	.4	.2	32.0
Total	$65.7	68.4	56.6	46.9	44.1	38.0	11.6
Operating Profits ($Millions)							
Thoroughbred Racing	$7.5	7.9	6.8	6.7	5.8	5.0	8.5%
Commercial Development	5.6	5.5	3.5	2.1	1.9	2.0	22.9
Real Estate Investments	1.2	.9	.9	.7	.4	—	31.6
Other	.7	.3	.2	.4	.3	.1	47.6
Total	$15.0	14.6	11.4	9.9	8.4	7.1	16.1

Source: Santa Anita Consolidated, Inc.'s annual reports for 1978 and 1979.

[1]Primarily from investment in Santa Anita Fashion Park.
[2]Primarily interest from money market investments.

commercial development, had grown at approximately the same rate. Operating profits had grown much faster for the commercial development business as compared to the thoroughbred racing operations. It is interesting to note that while real estate and other investments represented a relatively small portion of total revenues (3 percent in 1979), they represented a much larger portion of operating profits (13 percent in 1979). In addition, revenues and operating profits from these investments had grown much faster than the racing and commercial development businesses.

The decline in total revenues and commercial development revenues from 1978 to 1979 reflected Santa Anita Development's new operating philosophy of greater retention of properties for investment. Management felt that this decline was more than offset by the increased cash flow and market value associated with the retained properties.

Because of growing operating profits and cash flows, management adopted a regular quarterly dividend of 12.5 cents per common share which was paid in November 1977, February 1978, and May 1978. Also, an extra dividend of 10 cents per share was paid in May 1978. Subsequently, the regular quarterly dividend of 12.5 cents was increased to 15 cents in July 1978 and then, because of improved profit performance, was increased again to 25 cents the following quarter.

The change in operating philosophy of Santa Anita Development was expected to support this dividend policy by creating a consistent source of cash flow from rental income on the retained properties.

PLAN OF REORGANIZATION

According to Royce B. McKinley, Chief Executive Officer and a Director of Realty, Santa Anita's executives were seeking a means of increasing income available to stockholders. Originally, a tax-free reorganization was considered. But, subsequent analysis indicated that a tax-free reorganization would not accomplish the desired result. Since Santa Anita had large land holdings and derived significant income from these holdings, it was decided that a REIT form of organization would be an appropriate vehicle for distributing more income to stockholders.

A team consisting of the firm's investment banker, lawyers, and outside accountants was formed to hammer out the details of the reorganization. Accordingly, on August 20, 1979, Santa Anita announced the adoption by the Board of Directors of a plan of reorganization which called for converting part of the firm into a REIT. The reorganization required that Santa Anita Consolidated, Inc. be merged into a Delaware corporation in a share for share exchange. The new corporation, called Santa Anita Realty Enterprises, would operate as a REIT. The new REIT would own most of the real estate of Santa Anita, including the race track property at Santa Anita

Park, Santa Anita's interest in Santa Anita Fashion Park, and a portfolio of neighborhood shopping centers in California and Arizona. A separate Delaware corporation called Santa Anita Operating Company would conduct existing racing activities through Los Angeles Turf Club and commercial real estate development activities through Santa Anita Development. The shares of this company would be distributed as a dividend to Realty's shareholders. A copy of the plan of reorganization is provided in Appendix C. A detailed chronology of the steps followed in completing the spin-off is presented in Appendix D.

To maintain common ownership of Realty and Operating Company, the shares of the two firms would be "paired" so that such shares would be transferable only as units. To facilitate the pairing, Santa Anita stock certificates would be exchanged for new "back-to-back" certificates evidencing the stock of both Realty and Operating Company. In other words, the Realty stock certificate would be printed on the reverse of the Operating Company certificate. Management believed that the pairing was necessary because the two firms would have a close business relationship and questions of corporate opportunity and conflict of interest inherent in such a relationship would be reduced by common ownership.

Figure 9.1 illustrates the relationship between Santa Anita and its subsidiaries before and after the reorganization.

The purpose of merging Santa Anita into Realty was to facilitate the pairing. To pair effectively, each company must have a prohibition in its charter or by-laws on any transfers of shares other than in combination with an equal number of shares of the other company. Under California law, Santa Anita could not adopt such a restriction by means of an amendment to its charter or by-laws that would bind nonconsenting stockholders. Because the by-laws of Realty had a restriction on such transfers, the merger would accomplish this objective.

For Realty to qualify as a REIT, it would have to distribute to its shareholders annually at least 95 percent of its net income. No federal income tax would be payable by Realty on that income distributed to its shareholders, but Realty would pay corporate income tax on any amounts not distributed. Realty would also pay corporate income tax at a rate of 100 percent on net profits derived from the sale of property held for sale to customers in the ordinary course of its trade or business. Because of its status as a REIT, Realty would be able to pay a greater portion of its income as dividends to shareholders than Santa Anita was able to pay. If Realty did not qualify as a REIT, it would be taxed at ordinary corporate income tax rates on all income.

To qualify as a REIT, Realty was required to meet other statutory requirements relative to the nature of its investments and the source of its income. Generally, a REIT must invest at least 75 percent of its total assets

Figure 9.1
Santa Anita and Its Subsidiaries: Before and After Reorganization

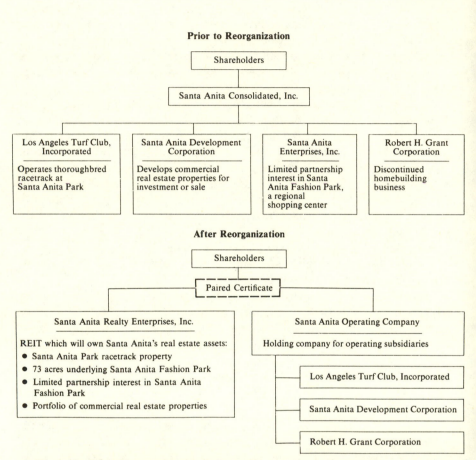

Prior to Reorganization

Shareholders

Santa Anita Consolidated, Inc.

Los Angeles Turf Club, Incorporated	Santa Anita Development Corporation	Santa Anita Enterprises, Inc.	Robert H. Grant Corporation
Operates thoroughbred racetrack at Santa Anita Park	Develops commercial real estate properties for investment or sale	Limited partnership interest in Santa Anita Fashion Park, a regional shopping center	Discontinued homebuilding business

After Reorganization

Shareholders

Paired Certificate

Santa Anita Realty Enterprises, Inc.

REIT which will own Santa Anita's real estate assets:
- Santa Anita Park racetrack property
- 73 acres underlying Santa Anita Fashion Park
- Limited partnership interest in Santa Anita Fashion Park
- Portfolio of commercial real estate properties

Santa Anita Operating Company

Holding company for operating subsidiaries

Los Angeles Turf Club, Incorporated

Santa Anita Development Corporation

Robert H. Grant Corporation

It is anticipated that after the Reorganization the shares of Santa Anita Realty Enterprises, Inc. and Santa Anita Operating Company will trade under the name Santa Anita Enterprises.

Pairing. To maintain common ownership of Realty and Operating Company after the Effective Time, shares of Realty Common Stock will be "paired" with Operating Company Common Shares so that such shares will be transferable and tradeable only as units of the same number of shares. Management believes that the Pairing is advisable because Realty and Operating Company will continue to have a close business relationship and questions of corporate opportunity and conflicts of interest inherent in such a relationship will be minimized by common ownership. See "The Reorganization—Pairing." In order to facilitate the Pairing, Santa Anita stock certificates will be exchanged for new "back-to-back" certificates evidencing the stock of both Realty and Operating Company.

Source: Santa Anita Consolidated Proxy Statement, p. 3.

in real estate assets, must derive at least 75 percent of its total income from real estate related investments, and must meet specific passivity requirements as to the nature of its operations.

The reorganization changed the rights of stockholders in the following ways:

1. Imposed restrictions on the transferability of the Realty common stock and Operating Company common stock because of the pairing.

2. If it is to qualify as a REIT, Realty may not own 10 percent or more of the outstanding common stock of Operating Company. If an individual owned 10 percent of Realty and 10 percent of Operating Company, that individual's ownership of Operating Company would be attributed to Realty. Hence, the by-laws of Realty and Operating Company prevent any shareholder from obtaining an ownership interest in either the voting power or total number of outstanding Operating Company common shares which would result in Realty being deemed to own more than 9.8 percent of the outstanding operating Company common shares. At the time of the reorganization, two directors together held more than 22 percent of Santa Anita common stock. Santa Anita entered into an agreement with these individuals to put part of their Operating Company shares in trust (for additional details see the prospectus).

3. The laws of Delaware differ from those of California (details are provided in the proxy statement).

Disadvantages associated with the pairing are as follows:

1. Realty may not be able to use its common stock to make acquisitions that are tax-free.

2. Neither Realty nor Operating Company will be able to issue shares of capital stock except in combination with shares of like securities in the other company.

3. A portion of the consideration received from any paired issuance will have to be allocated and paid to each company based on the relative values of the securities issued even though one company may have a greater need for capital than the other.

4. Each company will incur higher expenses as a result of its separate status including increased property management fees, increased stock transfer costs, increased auditing and legal fees, and increased reporting expenses.

5. Financing for either of the companies may be more difficult or costly because borrowing upon the combined income, cash flows, and assets of the two firms may not be possible.

Santa Anita's common stock was publicly held and traded over-the-counter. After the reorganization, the Realty common stock and the Operating Company common stock were listed on the New York Stock Exchange and traded only in units under the name Santa Anita Realty Enterprises.

Both stocks were required to be registered under the Securities Act of 1934 and were subject to the reporting, proxy, solicitation, and other requirements imposed by that statute on registered companies.

Significant dates and events associated with the reorganization and Realty's dividend policy are shown in Table 9.2.

The substantial increase in cash dividends in 1980 as compared to 1979 was a result of the reorganization and the reduction in federal income taxes associated with the REIT status of Realty.

Mr. McKinley stated that the reorganization was well received by stockholders and the investment community. Prior to the reorganization, stock in the two companies sold for approximately $13 per share. In early 1983, the paired stock traded in the range of $18-$19. The pairing agreement did not have any noticeable negative impact on the two firms. According to Mr. McKinley, fears concerning the ability of the two firms to obtain additional financing proved to be unfounded. Realty has had no difficulty in maintaining its REIT status. Because Realty is required to distribute 95 percent of its earnings as dividends to maintain its REIT status, Realty has not been able to retain earnings for growth. As a partial solution, Realty instituted a dividend reinvestment program.

A recent development has made the type of reorganization undertaken by Santa Anita more difficult to consummate. The Internal Revenue Service ruled that forming a REIT where the businesses of the two companies

Table 9.2
Significant Dates and Events Associated with Santa Anita's Reorganization

October 1978	Quarterly dividend rate raised to 12½ cents per quarter
April 1979	Public announcement of plans to form a REIT
August 1979	Board of Directors approve plan of reorganization
October 1979	Company receives favorable ruling from IRS
December 1979	Stockholders of Santa Anita approved the plan of reorganization
January 1980	Santa Anita Realty Enterprises Inc., and Santa Anita Operating Company are activated
February 1980	Realty declares regular quarterly dividend of 32½ cents
June 1980	Regular quarterly dividend raised to 35 cents
December 1980	Companies announce 100% stock dividend. Realty raises regular quarterly dividend to 38 cents.

Source: The Santa Anita Companies 1980 Annual Report.

would be integrated would be viewed unfavorably. The Internal Revenue Service's concern was the difficulty of analyzing intercompany transactions that occur on a contractual basis. Pairing of the stock was considered to be reflective of integration. Mr. McKinley felt that Santa Anita would not have pursued the plan of reorganization had the Internal Revenue Service not given a favorable ruling.

FEDERAL INCOME TAX CONSEQUENCES

To qualify as a REIT under Section 856 through 860 of the Internal Revenue Code of 1954, Realty must meet the following requirements as stated in the prospectus dated July 30, 1981:

(1) At least 95% of Realty's gross income (exclusive of gains from the sale of property held primarily for sale to customers in the ordinary course of its trade or business, other than foreclosure property) must be derived from:

    (a) rents from real property;

    (b) gain from the sale or disposition of real property that is not held primarily for sale to customers in the ordinary course of business;

    (c) interest on obligations secured by mortgages on real property (with certain minor exceptions);

    (d) dividends or other distributions on, and gains from the sale of, shares of qualified real estate investment trusts not held primarily for sale to customers in the ordinary course of business;

    (e) abatements and refunds of real property taxes;

    (f) income and gain derived from foreclosure property;

    (g) most types of commitment fees;

    (h) gains from sales or dispositions of real estate assets that qualify for exclusions from "prohibited transactions" under the Code;

    (i) dividends;

    (j) interest on other types of obligations (with certain minor exceptions); and

    (k) gains from sales or dispositions of securities not held primarily for sale to customers in the ordinary course of business.

Source: The Santa Anita Companies Prospectus dated July 30, 1981.

At least 75 percent of Realty's gross income, exclusive of gains from the sale of property held primarily for sale to customers in the ordinary course of its trade or business, (other than foreclosed property) must be derived from items (a) through (h).

(2) Less than 30% of Realty's gross income during any taxable year must be derived from the sale or disposition of (i) stock or securities held for less than one year; (ii) property held primarily for sale to customers in the ordinary course of business (other than foreclosure property); and (iii) real property (including interests in mortgages on real property) held for less than four years (other than foreclosure property and gains arising from involuntary conversions).

(3) At the end of each calendar quarter, at least 75% of the value of Realty's total assets must consist of real estate assets (real property, interests in real property, interests in mortgages on real property and shares in qualified real estate investment trusts), cash and cash items (including receivables) and government securities. In addition, with respect to securities that are not included in the 75% asset class, Realty may not at the end of any calendar quarter own (i) securities representing more than 10% of the outstanding voting securities of any one issuer or (ii) securities of any one issuer having a value that is more than 5% of the value of Realty's total assets. Assets held or income earned by a partnership in which Realty is a partner will be characterized by Realty in the same manner as they are characterized by the partnership for purposes of the requirements with respect to assets and income described above.

(4) The shares of Realty must be "transferable" and beneficial ownership of them must be held by 100 or more persons during at least 335 days of the taxable year. More than 50% of the outstanding stock may not be owned, directly or indirectly, actually or constructively, at any time during the last half of any taxable year by or for five or fewer "individuals," which include pension funds and certain other tax-exempt entities.

(5) Realty must distribute to its stockholders dividends in an amount at least equal to the sum of 95% of its "real estate investment trust taxable income" before deduction of dividends paid (less any net long-term capital gain and less any net income from foreclosure property or from property held primarily for sale to customers, plus any net loss from property held primarily for sale to customers and subject to certain other adjustments provided in the Code); *plus* (i) 95% of the excess of the net income from foreclosure property over the tax imposed on such income by the Code; *less* (ii) the sum of any tax penalty attributable to deficiency dividends paid by Realty and net losses from prohibited transactions. During 1980 Realty distributed 95% of its REIT taxable income.

(6) The directors of Realty must have exclusive authority over the management of Realty, the conduct of its affairs and, with certain limitations, the management and disposition of Realty's property.

(7) Realty must adopt the calendar year as its annual accounting period.

(8) Realty must satisfy certain procedural requirements.

The Code imposes a 100% tax on the net gain derived from the sale of property (other than "foreclosure property") held primarily for sale. Excluded from this tax are gains from the sale of real property, including shares in qualified real estate investment trusts, satisfying the following conditions, among others:

(a) the property has been held by Realty for at least four years;

(b) total capital expenditures with respect to the property during the four-year period prior to sale do not exceed 20% of the net selling price of the property;

(c) Realty does not make more than five sales of properties (other than "foreclosure property") during the taxable year; and

(d) if the property has not been acquired through foreclosure, the property is held by Realty for the production of rental income for at least four years.

This chapter described the reorganization and spin-off which transformed Santa Anita Consolidated, Inc. into Santa Anita Operating Company and Santa Anita Realty Enterprises, a real estate investment trust. Following the spin-off, shares of Santa Anita Operating Company and Santa Anita Realty Enterprises were paired and traded only as units. As a result of the reorganization and creation of the real estate investment trust, Santa Anita significantly reduced its federal income taxes.

Summary and Conclusions **10**

This chapter provides a brief summary of the important aspects of each of the preceding chapters. But before beginning this summary, it may be appropriate to attempt a more comprehensive overall assessment of the subject of corporate spin-offs.

This book provides the basis for an assessment of the efficacy of corporate spin-offs as a corporate strategic planning tool. The usefulness of corporate spin-offs for accomplishing a variety of corporate objectives has been illustrated with specific examples in Chapter 2. Chapters 3 and 4 have shown various technical aspects of spin-offs which must be dealt with by managements undertaking spin-offs. Chapter 5 has shown that when used wisely, a corporate spin-off can generate substantial profits for shareholders. But spin-offs are not suitable for solving every corporate problem. Chapter 8 describes the spin-off of Pengo Industries by Gearhart-Owen Industries. The purpose of the spin-off was to resolve managerial differences. This case represents one in which an alternate solution may have been more appropriate.

Corporate spin-offs are not a new managerial tool. Indeed, probably the first corporate spin-off was undertaken by Standard Oil in 1911. But the variety of situations in which spin-offs have been found to be useful has continued to grow. As business problems become more complex and managers become more sophisticated, it is likely that the use of spin-offs will continue to increase.

Chapter 1 defines what is meant by the term "corporate spin-off" and provides an introduction. In addition, the spin-off by American Telephone and Telegraph Company of seven regional operating companies is described. The American Telephone spin-off is the largest in history. Chapter 2 explores the reasons which have been given by corporate managers for undertaking spin-offs. Spin-offs have been used to (1) solve managerial problems, (2) correct difficulties arising from the capital markets, (3) control corporate risk, (4) achieve tax benefits, (5) accomplish marketing objectives, and (6-7) overcome regulatory and legal problems. Each of these objectives is illustrated with several specific examples, which are included to describe the variety of situations in which spin-offs are useful.

Chapter 3 describes mechanical aspects of corporate spin-offs. A wide variety of topics including the plan of reorganization, which is a part of every spin-off, the proxy statement, and the registration statement, are described. Information is provided concerning the transfers of assets and employees, adjustments for stock options, warrants and convertibles, arrangements for pension plans, and the employment of experts and other matters. The chapter tells how to obtain documents from the Securities and Exchange Commission concerning spin-offs of other corporations which may be of interest to executives planning a spin-off.

Chapter 4 discusses the accounting and tax aspects of corporate spin-offs. The applications of Accounting Principles Board Opinion No. 29, "Accounting for Nonmonetary Transactions," and Accounting Principles Board Opinion No. 30, "Reporting the Results of Operations," are described. Specific examples which illustrate the application of these Accounting Principles Board Opinions using both actual and hypothetical data are provided.

Chapter 4 also describes the tax treatment of spin-offs. In most cases, spin-offs qualify as tax-free reorganizations. This chapter outlines the requirements necessary to achieve this tax-free status. But even when this tax-free treatment is not available, the benefits of the spin-off may be more than sufficient to justify the spin-off. The spin-off which occurred in connection with the formation of The Santa Anita Companies described in Chapter 9 is an example of just such a case.

Chapter 5 describes the economic consequences of corporate spin-offs. It is assumed that managements would not undertake voluntary spin-offs unless they expected them to increase shareholder wealth. Hence, the main focus of the chapter is to ascertain whether these expected increases in shareholder wealth, in fact, did materialize. Two academic studies and one security industry study are examined in detail. These studies use techniques which differ greatly in approach, but agree that voluntary corporate spin-offs typically have increased shareholder wealth. The impact of larger spin-offs on shareholder wealth was found to be larger than that of smaller spin-offs. These conclusions hold even when the differing risk of the corporations involved and the differing performance of the stock market as a whole at various points in time are taken into account.

Chapters 6, 7, 8, and 9 are each devoted to individual case studies of spin-offs. The particular spin-offs examined were selected because they illustrate a wide variety of situations which lead to corporate spin-offs. In addition, of course, it was necessary to choose spin-offs for which sufficient publicly accessible information was available. These chapters include useful information supplied by interviews with executives at the companies actually involved in these spin-offs. These executives were asked to answer a number of questions such as the following: (1) Were there any unanticipated problems resulting from the spin-off? (2) What was the reaction of stockholders and the financial community to the spin-off? (3) What was the reaction of employees to the spin-off? (4) How did the spin-off affect corporate executives? and (5) What advice would they give other executives contemplating a spin-off?

The first case study describes the various spin-offs undertaken by Tandy Corporation. In 1975 Tandy Corporation spun off Tandycrafts, Inc. and Tandy Brands, Inc. Subsequently, Tandycrafts spun off Stafford-Lowdon in 1976 and Color Tile in 1979. The purpose of all of these spin-offs was to increase managerial efficiency. For example, by establishing separate companies, an improved reward structure could be created. The chapter includes a list of the various firms spun-off and sold by Tandy from 1974 to 1982. A detailed discussion of how Tandy management decided between a spin-off and a sale is provided.

Chapter 7 describes the spin-off of Louisiana-Pacific Corporation from Georgia-Pacific Corporation in early 1973. The Georgia-Pacific case is the only one of the four which describes an involuntary spin-off. Since in the case of involuntary spin-offs management is forced to undertake the spin-off, it is assumed that management anticipates that the spin-off will have a negative impact on shareholder wealth. This chapter is devoted to an analysis of whether such a negative impact on shareholder wealth occurred for this spin-off. The results show that following the spin-off Georgia-Pacific experienced a decline in the rate of return of its shares relative to the market. Further, the risk of Georgia-Pacific as measured by beta (a measure of the risk that a stock shares with the market) increased following the spin-off.

Chapter 8 describes the spin-off of Pengo Industries, Inc. from Gearhart-Owen Industries, Inc. The purpose of the spin-off was to resolve differences which had developed between Mr. Gearhart and Mr. Owen, the two founders of the business, concerning the firm's investment policies. Mr. Gearhart wanted to focus exclusively on wireline services which were provided to the oil industry while Mr. Owen believed that the firm had sufficient funds to expand in both the wireline services industry and in other industries in which the company operated. Relations between Gearhart-Owen's senior executives became so strained that the Board of Directors proposed the spin-off to restore management harmony. But since the spin-off, the managements of both Gearhart-Owen and Pengo have had second thoughts about the appropriateness of a spin-off to resolve management differences.

The final case examined in detail in Chapter 9 is the reorganization and spin-off undertaken by Santa Anita Consolidated, Inc. The principal purpose of the spin-off was to reduce substantially the firm's federal income taxes. This was achieved by separating the firm into real estate and other operations. After the reorganization and spin-off, income from the real estate holdings flowed to stockholders through a real estate investment trust and was not subject to federal corporate income tax.

APPENDIXES

Easco Corporation—Notice of Special Meeting of Stockholders

EASCO CORPORATION

BALTIMORE, MARYLAND

October 7, 1972

To the Voting Stockholders:

A special meeting of the stockholders of Easco Corporation will be held on October 31, 1972, at the Hollyday Room, One Village Square, The Village of Cross Keys, 5100 Falls Road, Baltimore, Maryland to consider and act upon a Plan of Reorganization (the "Plan") that will result in the distribution to Easco common stockholders of the Common Stock of a new corporation, Eastmet Corporation ("Eastmet"). As part of the Plan, Easco will, prior to the distribution, transfer to Eastmet the Eastern Stainless Steel Company Division of Easco and the stock of Philipp Overseas Incorporated and Industrial Service Centers, Inc.

If the Plan is approved, one share of Common Stock of Eastmet will be distributed in respect of each two shares of Easco Common Stock. In the view of the directors, the Plan will give maximum recognition to, and take better advantage of, the separate and distinct operating, financial and investment characteristics of two major areas of Easco's business. It is believed that both companies will benefit, and that Eastmet will be able to pursue opportunities to strengthen its position as a successful producer and distributor of stainless steel sheet and plate and expand its related international metals trading business. Easco will continue with the same name, and its Common Stock will be traded as at present on the New York Stock Exchange. Its businesses immediately after the distribution will consist of four major operating groups: hand tools and forged products; technical services; aluminum products; and industrial components.

The directors believe that each company will have strong and capable management after the transaction. John M. Curley, Jr., Chairman of Easco, will become Chairman and President of Eastmet. Edward J. Donnelly, Vice-Chairman of Easco, will become Chairman of Easco, and Richard P. Sullivan, currently President of Easco, will continue in that position. Mr. Curley will continue as an Easco director and Mr. Donnelly will become a director of Eastmet. Otherwise, the Boards of Directors of the two companies are to be separate, as described in the proxy statement.

The proposals have been recommended after full consideration by your directors. We urge you to study the proposals carefully and, on behalf of the Board of Directors, solicit your proxy authorizing a favorable vote thereon. Please sign and return the accompanying proxy in the enclosed addressed envelope. Any stockholder who desires to vote in person may, if he wishes, withdraw his proxy and cast his vote personally if he attends the meeting.

Sincerely yours,
JOHN M. CURLEY, JR.
Chairman of the Board

EDWARD J. DONNELLY
Vice Chairman of the Board

EASCO CORPORATION

BALTIMORE, MARYLAND

———————

Notice of Special Meeting of Stockholders
to be held October 31, 1972

———————

To the holders of Common Stock
and Series B Preferred Stock:

A Special Meeting of the Stockholders of Easco Corporation will be held at the Hollyday Room, One Village Square, The Village of Cross Keys, 5100 Falls Road, Baltimore, Maryland, at 10:00 a.m., Baltimore time, on October 31, 1972 (a) for the purpose of considering and acting upon a Plan of Reorganization dated as of August 31, 1972 (the "Plan") providing for (i) the transfer of the assets of the Eastern Stainless Steel Company Division of Easco and the stocks of Philipp Overseas Incorporated and Industrial Service Centers, Inc., to Eastmet Corporation ("Eastmet"), (ii) the ancillary transfer of stock of other Easco subsidiaries to a new intermediate holding company, (iii) the distribution of Eastmet Common Stock to the common stockholders of Easco, and (iv) related adjustments to employee benefit plans and other matters incident to the Plan; and (b) to transact such other business as may properly come before the meeting.

The close of business on September 29, 1972 has been fixed as the record date for the determination of the stockholders entitled to notice of and to vote at such meeting. The stock transfer books will not be closed.

Stockholders are urged to sign, date and return the enclosed proxy as soon as possible. A postpaid envelope is enclosed for that purpose.

By Order of the Board of Directors,

DAVID L. KAUFFMAN,
Secretary.

October 7, 1972

Table of Contents

INTRODUCTION AND SUMMARY

The following is a brief summary of some of the essential features of the proposed transaction. The summary is not intended to be a complete statement of all material features of the proposal, and is qualified in its entirety by reference to the more detailed statements in the body of the proxy statement.

Purpose of Meeting

The purpose of the meeting is to consider and act on the transfers of Easco assets to two separate corporations, for the purpose of establishing Eastmet Corporation as a separate corporate entity to be followed by the distribution by Easco to its stockholders of one share of Common Stock of Eastmet for each two shares of Common Stock of Easco.

Easco and Eastmet Businesses

If the Plan is approved, Easco and Eastmet will be separate corporations conducting the following respective lines of businesses:

Easco	Eastmet
Hand Tools and Forged Products	Stainless Mill Products
Aluminum Products	Metals Service Centers
Industrial Components	International Operations
Technical Services	

The Board of Directors has concluded that the separation of the lines of businesses to create two separate independent stockholder owned corporations is necessary and desirable to permit the respective lines of businesses to meet their increased capital demands and to provide a basis for the expansion and pursuit of the corporate objectives of the respective lines of businesses. See "Reasons for the Reorganization" and "Easco After the Separation" and "Eastmet After the Separation" under "Business and Properties of Easco".

Distribution of Eastmet Stock

If the Plan is approved at the meeting, and subject to the satisfaction of all other conditions of the Plan, one share of the Eastmet Common Stock will be distributed in respect of each two shares of Easco Common Stock held. It is now anticipated that the distribution will be to holders of record of Easco Common Stock on November 15, 1972, and that the distribution will be made on or about November 30, 1972. Easco stockholders will receive notice of the satisfaction of all conditions and the final dates established.

Easco Common Stock will continue to be listed on the New York Stock Exchange. It is anticipated that Eastmet Common Stock will be traded in the over-the-counter market.

Comparative Per Share Data

The following shows the historical earnings per share of Easco Common Stock for the periods noted, on a fully diluted basis, together with pro forma data for the same periods for Easco and Eastmet after the separation:

	Year ended December 31, 1971	Six months ended June 30, 1971	1972
Easco Corporation-Historical			
Fully diluted earnings per share:			
Income before extraordinary items	$1.45	$ .79	$ .92
Extraordinary items	(.52)	—	—
Net income	$ .93	$ .79	$ .92
Pro forma after the separation			
Eastmet Corporation			
Pro forma earnings per share adjusted for prospective interest rate:			
Income before extraordinary items	$ .76	$ .90	$ .49
Net income (loss)	($ .49)	$ .90	$ .49

	Year ended December 31, 1971	Six months ended June 30, 1971	1972
Easco Corporation (excluding Eastmet)			
Pro forma earnings per share adjusted for prospective interest rate:			
Fully diluted _____	$1.06	$ .36	$ .67

See "Comparative Per Share Data".

Dividends

The Board of Directors of Easco has determined and provided in the Plan that the historical cash dividends of Easco on its Common Stock should be allocated one-half to Easco and one-half to Eastmet in determining the accounting basis for the separation. The most recent Easco cash dividend, payable October 2, 1972 to stockholders of record September 15, 1972 was 12½¢ per share. Under such allocation, the amounts would have been 6¼¢ per one Easco common share and 12½¢ per one Eastmet common share. Provision is made in the Plan for the appropriate adjustments to avoid any abnormalities in the normal schedule of dividends due to the Plan. Both companies intend to consider dividend action on a quarterly basis, and future dividends will depend on the financial condition, earnings and capital needs of the companies. See "Accounting; Dividend Coordination".

Assets and Capitalization

The following shows the long-term debt, the shareholders equity, and book value per share of Common Stock for Easco historically and for Eastmet and Easco after the separation, on a pro forma basis, as of June 30, 1972:

	(thousands except per share data)		
	Easco Historical	Successor Corporations Easco	Eastmet
Long-term debt _____	$25,279	$15,529	$10,500
Shareholders Equity _____	$60,679	$30,772	$29,907
Book Value per Common Share			
(before conversion of preferred stock) _____ _____	$ 18.64	$ 7.05	$ 23.68

See "Capitalization", "Comparative Per Share Data" and "Consolidated and Pro Forma Balance Sheet".

Federal Tax Consequences

Easco has applied for a ruling from the Commissioner of Internal Revenue generally to the effect that the transactions under the Plan will be tax-free to the companies and to the stockholders of Easco. The transaction is conditioned upon receipt of a favorable ruling to such effect. See "Federal Income Tax Consequences".

Treatment of Convertible Preferred Stock

Under the terms of the outstanding convertible preferred stocks of Easco, adjustments will take place increasing the numbers of shares of Common Stock into which each share of the convertible preferred stocks is convertible to make appropriate adjustments for the value of the Eastmet Common Stock distributed to the Easco common stockholders. Holders of the Easco convertible preferred stocks have the right to convert their shares into Common Stock prior to the record date for the distribution, and thereby to participate in the distribution as holders of Easco Common Stock. In the absence of such conversions, holders of the convertible preferred stocks will receive the benefit of the adjustment described above but will not receive a distribution of Eastmet shares. See "Convertible Preferred Stock Adjustments".

Voting Rights; Appraisal Rights

The Plan will require the approval of a majority of the votes entitled to be cast at the meeting in order to be adopted, with all outstanding Easco voting shares voting together as a single class. Holders of Easco Common Stock will have no appraisal rights. Holders of Easco convertible preferred stocks will have appraisal rights; however, such rights arise only by virtue of the use of certain features of the Plan which may be eliminated by the Easco Board of Directors if indicated exercises of appraisal rights would jeopardize the transaction or be detrimental to the companies. Accordingly, there may be no appraisal rights for any stockholders in the transaction. See "Rights of Dissent".

APPENDIX

Facet Enterprises, Inc.— Prospectus

FACET ENTERPRISES, INC.

3,016,320 Shares

Common Stock ($1 par value)

On or about April 1, 1976, The Bendix Corporation will distribute to its Common Stockholders of record on March 18, 1976, 3,016,320 shares of Common Stock of Facet Enterprises, Inc., a wholly-owned subsidiary of Bendix, as a dividend on the basis of one full share of Facet Common Stock for each five shares of Bendix Common Stock. No fractional share certificates or scrip will be issued. (See "The Distribution" below.) Neither Bendix nor Facet will receive any cash or other proceeds in connection with the distribution.

Bendix owns 3,330,000 shares of Facet Common Stock. The shares not required for the distribution will be contributed by Bendix to Facet. Accordingly, after the distribution and such contribution, Bendix will own no Facet stock.

The Bendix Salaried Employees' Savings and Stock Ownership Plan trust fund will receive, as a Common Stockholder of Bendix, approximately 16% of the shares of Facet Common Stock being distributed. (See "Principal Stockholders" below.)

Facet's application for the listing of its Common Stock on the New York Stock Exchange has been approved. "When issued" trading in Facet Common Stock on such Exchange is expected to commence on or after March 24, 1976.

This distribution has been registered under the Securities Act of 1933 because in the view of the Securities and Exchange Commission Bendix may be deemed to be an "underwriter" with respect to the distribution within the meaning of Section 2(11) of such Act.

THESE SECURITIES HAVE NOT BEEN APPROVED OR DISAPPROVED BY THE SECURITIES AND EXCHANGE COMMISSION NOR HAS THE COMMISSION PASSED UPON THE ACCURACY OR ADEQUACY OF THIS PROSPECTUS. ANY REPRESENTATION TO THE CONTRARY IS A CRIMINAL OFFENSE.

The date of this Prospectus is March 22, 1976.

No dealer or other person has been authorized to give any information or to make any representation in connection with the distribution of shares to which this Prospectus relates other than those contained herein and, if given or made, such information or representation must not be relied upon as having been authorized by Facet or Bendix. Neither the delivery of this Prospectus nor any transaction effected hereunder shall under any circumstances create an implication that there has been no change in the affairs of Facet since the date hereof. This Prospectus does not constitute an offer or solicitation by anyone in any state in which such offer or solicitation is not authorized or in which the person making such offer or solicitation is not qualified to do so or to anyone to whom it is unlawful to make such offer or solicitation.

Until June 21, 1976, all dealers effecting transactions in the shares to which this Prospectus relates may be required to deliver a Prospectus. Copies of this Prospectus may be obtained from Facet at its offices at 7030 South Yale Avenue, Tulsa, Oklahoma 74136.

TABLE OF CONTENTS

PROSPECTUS SUMMARY

The following summary is qualified in its entirety by the detailed information and financial statements (including the notes thereto) appearing elsewhere in this Prospectus.

FACET ENTERPRISES, INC.

Facet principally manufactures and sells a wide range of filters and automotive components. It also develops and manufactures environmental waste treatment equipment. Manufacturing is primarily conducted at seven filter plants and two automotive components plants. Facet also has numerous warehouses and sales offices throughout the United States and in Canada.

Sole Stockholder .... The Bendix Corporation

History of Business .... Facet is the successor to certain businesses formerly owned by Bendix and its subsidiary, Fram Corporation, which were transferred to Facet in 1975 pursuant to an order of the Federal Trade Commission.

THE DISTRIBUTION

Type and Amount of Security .... 3,016,320 shares of Facet Common Stock

Listing .... New York Stock Exchange

Method of Distribution .... Dividend to holders of Bendix Common Stock on the record date on the basis of one share of Facet Common Stock for each five shares of Bendix Common Stock

Record Date .... March 18, 1976

Date of Distribution .... On or about April 1, 1976

Reason for Distribution .... Bendix must dispose of its interest in Facet to comply with an order of the Federal Trade Commission.

SELECTED FINANCIAL INFORMATION

(All figures in thousands, except per share data)

	Year Ended September 30		Three Months Ended December 31	
	1974	1975	1974	1975
Pro Forma Statement of Income(1):				
Net sales	$84,211	$90,261	$21,212	$23,552
Pro forma net income	3,377	2,150	900	198
Pro forma earnings per share(2)	1.12	.71	.30	.07

	September 30, 1975	December 31, 1975
Balance Sheet:		
Working capital	$31,225	$31,428
Land, buildings, and equipment — Net	13,877	13,932
Total assets	62,915	63,584
Long-term obligation under industrial revenue bonds	540	540
Stockholder's equity	46,903	47,101

(1) See Notes A and B to Pro Forma Consolidated Statement of Income.

(2) The pro forma earnings per share have been computed based upon 3,016,320 shares of Facet Common Stock, the number to be outstanding immediately after the distribution.

THE COMPANY

Facet Enterprises, Inc. ("Facet" or the "Company") principally manufactures and sells a wide range of filters and automotive components. It also develops and manufactures environmental waste treatment equipment. ("Facet" is an acronym for Filters, Automotive Components, Environmental Technology.)

Facet is the successor to several businesses (the oldest of which was established in 1883), which were transferred to it on March 31, 1975 by The Bendix Corporation ("Bendix") and its wholly-owned subsidiary, Fram Corporation ("Fram"), as a result of an order of the Federal Trade Commission ("FTC").

Facet was incorporated in Delaware on February 10, 1975. Its executive offices are located at 7030 South Yale Avenue, Tulsa, Oklahoma 74136 and its telephone number is (Area Code 918) 492-1800.

As used herein, the terms "Facet" or "Company" include Facet Enterprises, Inc., its predecessors as operations of Bendix and Fram, and its subsidiaries, unless the context otherwise requires.

DISPOSITION BY BENDIX

In June, 1967, Bendix acquired Fram, a manufacturer of replaceable oil, air and fuel filters for internal combustion engines, automobile engine fans, heating, ventilating and air conditioning filters and industrial filtration products. Immediately thereafter, the FTC brought an action challenging the legality of the acquisition under the antitrust laws and seeking to require Bendix to dispose of the Fram business and assets it had acquired.

The matter was litigated more than seven years until, on November 12, 1974, pursuant to an agreement with Bendix, the FTC issued an order (the "FTC Order"), which requires Bendix to dispose of certain operations and product lines owned by it or by Fram. To accomplish this disposition, Bendix formed a wholly-owned subsidiary (Facet), and on March 31, 1975 Bendix and Fram transferred to Facet the assets and related liabilities to be disposed of and granted to Facet certain licenses and rights relating to the transferred products. (See "Business — Automotive Components Group" and "Business — Patents, Trademarks and Licenses" below.) Under the FTC Order, Bendix must dispose of its interest in Facet prior to November 13, 1976.

As described above, Facet is the result of an agreement between Bendix and the FTC. The businesses and assets that are to be disposed of by Bendix and that consequently have been transferred to Facet were chosen after extensive negotiations with the FTC, in which there were many competing considerations. Unlike the typical company, the businesses and assets that make up Facet do not have their origin in a plan of acquisition or internal expansion created by management. (See "Business" and Note A to Pro Forma Consolidated Statement of Income below.)

These businesses and assets were transferred to Facet on March 31, 1975. Accordingly, although much of the information contained in this Prospectus treats Facet as though it has operated in its present form for the last three years, prior to March 31, 1975, these businesses and assets were operated as subsidiaries, divisions or parts of divisions of Bendix and Fram. (See Notes A and B to Pro Forma Consolidated Statement of Income below.) In addition, since Facet was only organized in 1975, its management has not yet been in office for a full fiscal year.

Santa Anita's Agreement and Plan of Reorganization, as amended [composite]

AGREEMENT AND PLAN OF REORGANIZATION, as amended
[composite]

This Agreement and Plan of Reorganization (the "Agreement") is entered into by and among Santa Anita Consolidated, Inc., a California corporation ("Santa Anita"), Santa Anita Realty Enterprises, Inc., a Delaware corporation ("Realty"), and Santa Anita Operating Company, a Delaware corporation ("Operating Company"), as of this first day of October, 1979, as amended as of the 15th day of November, 1979.

RECITALS

A. Realty and Operating Company are wholly-owned subsidiaries of Santa Anita; and

B. Santa Anita owns all of the issued and outstanding capital stock of Los Angeles Turf Club, Incorporated ("LATC"), Santa Anita Development Corporation ("SDC"), Santa Anita Enterprises, Inc. ("SAE") and Robert H. Grant Corporation ("Grant Corporation"), each of which is a California corporation; and

C. Santa Anita, Realty and Operating Company desire to adopt a plan of reorganization for the purpose of enabling Realty to qualify as a real estate investment trust ("REIT") under the Internal Revenue Code of 1954, as amended (the "Code"), which reorganization will be effected by (i) Santa Anita being merged into Realty pursuant to an Agreement of Merger (the "Merger Agreement"), substantially in the form of Exhibit A attached hereto (the "Merger"), (ii) all the common stock of Operating Company ("Operating Company Common Shares") being distributed to the shareholders of Realty (the "Distribution"), and (iii) the shares of Realty and Operating Company being paired together so that they will only be tradeable and transferable in units (the "Pairing"). The Merger, Distribution and Pairing shall be collectively referred to as the "Reorganization."

AGREEMENT

In order to consummate this Agreement and effect such Merger, Distribution and Pairing, the parties hereto agree as follows:

ARTICLE ONE

The Reorganization

1.1 In consideration of the agreements herein set forth, by the adoption of this Agreement and subject to the approval of this Agreement by the shareholder of Realty and Operating Company and the shareholders of Santa Anita, and subject to the conditions hereinafter set forth: (i) Santa Anita will contribute to Operating Company certain assets of Santa Anita which are inadvisable for a REIT to hold together with all of the outstanding capital stock of LATC, SDC and Grant Corporation, in exchange for that number of Operating Company Common Shares which, when added to the shares previously owned by Santa Anita, will equal the number of shares of Santa Anita issued and outstanding (less the number of Operating Company Common Shares to be waived pursuant to the agreement described in Section 1.8 hereof); and (ii) pursuant to the Merger Agreement Santa Anita will be merged with and into Realty, which will continue under the laws of Delaware as the company surviving the Merger (hereinafter sometimes referred to as the "Surviving Corporation"), the separate existence of Santa Anita will cease, and all of the property, assets, business and rights of Santa Anita (including the Operating Company Common Shares) will be vested in Realty, and all of the debts, liabilities and obligations of Santa Anita will become the debts, liabilities and obligations of Realty. The terms, provisions and obligations of the Merger of Santa Anita into Realty hereby agreed upon and the mode of carrying the same into effect shall be as set forth in the Merger Agreement.

1.2 The Certificate of Incorporation of the Surviving Corporation shall not hereby or otherwise be amended by reason of the effectiveness of the Merger and shall continue to be the Certificate of Incorporation of the Surviving Corporation until amended in accordance with the laws of Delaware and the provisions of such Certificate of Incorporation.

1.3 The by-laws of the Surviving Corporation, as in effect on the Effective Time (as hereinafter defined in Article Six of this Agreement), shall be and constitute the by-laws of the Surviving Corporation until the same shall be altered, amended or repealed or until new by-laws are adopted as provided by law, such by-laws or the Certificate of Incorporation of the Surviving Corporation.

1.4 At the Effective Time, the directors of Realty holding office immediately prior to the Effective Time shall become the directors of the Surviving Corporation and shall hold office for the term specified in the Certificate of Incorporation or by-laws of the Surviving Corporation, or until their successors are elected and qualify.

1.5 The officers of the Surviving Corporation immediately prior to the Effective Time of the Merger shall, when the Merger becomes effective, hold the same respective offices with the Surviving Corporation.

1.6 Subject to the effectiveness of the Merger, the Board of Directors of Santa Anita will declare a dividend in kind on the shares of its common stock, consisting of approximately 2,600,000 Operating Company Common Shares, $.10 par value, such number to be adjusted, if necessary, so as to equal the number of shares of Realty Common Stock outstanding when the Merger becomes effective less the number of shares specified in the agreement described in Section 1.8 hereof. The Operating Company Common Shares will be distributed in the ratio of one Operating Company Common Share for each outstanding share of common stock of Realty, $.10 par value ("Realty Common Stock"), which will become outstanding when the Merger becomes effective, subject to the agreement described in Section 1.8 hereof. The Distribution will be deemed for all purposes to have occurred at the close of business on the date of the Effective Time.

1.7 Realty and Operating Company will enter into a Pairing Agreement, dated as of December 31, 1979, (the "Pairing Agreement"), pursuant to which the shares of Realty Common Stock and the Operating Company Common Shares will be paired so that they are transferable and tradeable only in units, each unit consisting of an equal number of shares of Realty Common Stock and Operating Company Common Shares, subject to the agreement described in Section 1.8 hereof.

1.8 Santa Anita, Operating Company, Realty, Mr. Robert H. Grant and Mr. Richard L. Owen will enter into agreements satisfactory to the Board of Directors of Santa Anita, pursuant to which Mr. Grant and Mr. Owen will (i) transfer such amount of Operating Company Common Shares to third parties which transfers will result in Realty being deemed to own, under the attribution rules of the Code, less than 9.8% of the outstanding Operating Company Common Shares after the Distribution, (ii) agree not to sell the unpaired shares of Realty Common Stock received by them in the Merger except under certain circumstances and (iii) agree to certain other conditions.

ARTICLE TWO

Method of Effecting the Merger,
Distribution and Pairing

2.1 The mode of carrying the Merger Agreement into effect and the manner and basis of converting the shares of common stock, without par value, of Santa Anita ("Santa Anita Common Stock") into shares of Realty Common Stock shall be as follows:

(a) Each shareholder of Santa Anita who does not dissent to the Merger as provided in subparagraph (b) of this Paragraph 2.1 shall be bound by each and all of the provisions of this Agreement as if he shall have in person executed it.

(b) Any shareholder of Santa Anita who shall elect not to receive the shares of Realty Common Stock for his shares of Santa Anita Common Stock as hereinafter provided shall be bound by all of the requirements and shall have all and only the rights and remedies of a dissenting shareholder as provided in Sections 1300 through 1312 of the California Corporations Code, which are by reference incorporated herein.

(c) At the Effective Time, each issued and outstanding share of Santa Anita Common Stock (excluding shares held by those shareholders of Santa Anita who have taken action to perfect their dissenters' rights under subparagraph (b) of this Paragraph 2.1) shall by virtue of the Merger be converted into and become, without action on the part of the holder thereof, one fully paid and non-assessable share of Realty Common Stock.

(d) At the Effective Time, each outstanding option to purchase Santa Anita Common Stock shall by virtue of the Merger become an option to purchase from whichever of Realty or Operating Company the employment of the optionholder was attributed prior to the Reorganization the same number of shares of Realty Common Stock and, after the Distribution is effected, with respect to those options assumed by Operating Company, an equal number of Operating Company Common Shares, at the purchase price per share specified in said option.

(e) All shares of Realty Common Stock for which shares of Santa Anita Common Stock shall have been exchanged and converted pursuant to this Paragraph 2.1 shall be deemed to have been delivered and received in full satisfaction of all rights pertaining to such Santa Anita Common Stock.

(f) At the Effective Time, Realty shall possess all the rights, privileges, powers and franchises, of a public as well as a private nature, of Santa Anita, and all and singular the rights, privileges, powers and franchises of Santa Anita, and all property, real, personal and mixed, and all debts due to Santa Anita on whatever account, as well as for stock subscriptions and all other things in action or belonging to Santa Anita, shall be vested in Realty; and all property, assets, rights, privileges, powers, franchises and immunities, and all and every other interest shall be thereafter as effectually the property of Realty as they were of Santa Anita and the title to any real estate vested by deed or otherwise in Santa Anita shall not revert or be in any way impaired by reason of the Merger; provided, however, that all rights of creditors and all liens upon any property of Santa Anita shall be preserved and unimpaired, and all debts, liabilities, obligations and duties of Santa Anita shall thenceforth attach to Realty, and may be enforced against it to the same extent as if said debts, liabilities, obligations and duties had been incurred or contracted by it.

2.2 (a) As of the Effective Time, each Santa Anita stock certificate issued and not cancelled prior to that time which had represented shares of Santa Anita Common Stock (excluding shares held by those shareholders of Santa Anita who have taken action to perfect their dissenters' rights under subparagraph (b) of Paragraph 2.1) will be deemed to evidence for all corporate purposes, except as provided below, an equal number of shares of Realty Common Stock and Operating Company Common Shares, each holder of record of Santa Anita Common Stock will be registered on the stock records of Realty and Operating Company, respectively, as owning the number of shares of Realty Common Stock into which such shareholder's shares of Santa Anita Common Stock were converted in the Merger and the number of Operating Company Common Shares which were distributed to him in the Distribution, and each holder of a certificate or certificates which prior to the Effective Time represented shares of Santa Anita Common Stock shall, upon presentation of such certificate or certificates to Realty, Operating Company or Union Bank, Los Angeles, their exclusive exchange agent, be entitled to receive in exchange therefor a certificate or certificates representing the same number of shares of fully paid and nonassessable Realty Common Stock and Operating Company Common Shares; provided, however, that no dividends declared with respect to either the Realty Common Stock or the Operating Company Common Shares (other than the dividend of Operating Company Common Shares by Realty) shall be paid to the holder of any unsurrendered certificate of Santa Anita Common Stock until such holder shall surrender such certificate, at which time the holder shall be paid the amount of dividends, without interest, which theretofore were declared and became payable with respect to the number of shares of Realty Common Stock and Operating Company Common Shares evidenced by such certificate; and provided further that the foregoing shall be subject to the agreement described in Section 1.8 hereof.

(b) Notwithstanding Paragraph 2.2(a), as provided in the agreement described in Section 1.8 hereof, certificates representing the unpaired Realty Common Stock and the unpaired Operating Company Common Shares shall only be deemed to evidence, for all corporate purposes, the shares of stock of either Realty or Operating Company, as the case may be.

2.3 The Pairing will be effected in accordance with the provisions of the Pairing Agreement.

ARTICLE THREE

Covenants

3.1 Realty shall:

(a) Cause the issuance, at the appropriate time or times, of all of the shares of Realty Common Stock into which the shares of Santa Anita Common Stock are to be converted and exchanged.

(b) Use its best efforts to obtain from any regulatory authority having jurisdiction any and all qualifications required for the issuance and delivery of Realty Common Stock or other consummation of the other transactions contemplated by this Agreement.

(c) Assume those obligations under employment agreements, arrangements and plans of Santa Anita attributable to operations of Santa Anita to be continued by it.

(d) Assume as of the Effective Time, each option heretofore granted by Santa Anita pursuant to its Employee Incentive Stock Option Program and outstanding immediately prior to the Effective Time which is held by an individual whose employment, prior to the Effective Time, was attributable to the operations of Santa Anita to be conducted by Realty, after which assumption the terms of the option shall remain unchanged, except that the stock issuable upon the exercise thereof shall be a number of shares of Realty Common Stock which is the product of a percentage equal to the amount of the optionee's employment, prior to the Effective Time, attributable to operations to be conducted by Realty and the number of shares of Santa Anita Common Stock subject to the outstanding option.

(e) Use its best efforts to perform all of its covenants and to comply with all of the conditions to be complied with by it hereunder, and to take all other action necessary to complete the transaction provided for by this Agreement.

3.2 Santa Anita shall:

(a) Use its best efforts to obtain any and all necessary orders, consents and approvals from any regulatory authority having jurisdiction over the transaction contemplated by this Agreement.

(b) Use its best efforts to perform all of its covenants and to comply with all of the conditions to be complied with by it hereunder and to take all other action necessary to complete the transactions provided for by this Agreement.

3.3 Operating Company shall:

(a) Use its best efforts to obtain any and all necessary orders, consents and approvals from any regulatory authority having jurisdiction over the transaction contemplated by this Agreement.

(b) Assume those obligations under employment agreements, arrangements and plans of Santa Anita attributable to operations of Santa Anita to be continued by it.

(c) Assume, as of the Effective Time, each option heretofore granted by Santa Anita pursuant to its Employee Incentive Stock Option Program and outstanding immediately prior to the Effective Time which is held by an individual whose employment, prior to the Effective Time, was attributable to the operations of Santa Anita to be conducted by Operating Company, after which assumption the terms of the option shall remain unchanged, except that the stock issuable upon the exercise thereof shall be a number of Operating Company Common Shares which is the product of a percentage equal to the amount of the optionee's employment, prior to the Effective Time, attributable to operations to be conducted by Operating Company and the number of shares of Santa Anita Common Stock subject to the outstanding option, plus an equal number of shares of Realty Common Stock.

(d) Use its best efforts to perform all of its covenants and to comply with all of the conditions to be complied with by it hereunder and to take all other action necessary to complete the transaction provided for by this Agreement.

ARTICLE FOUR

Conditions

4.1 The consummation of the Reorganization provided for herein shall be subject to the following conditions:

(a) The holders of a majority of the outstanding Santa Anita Common Stock shall have voted in favor of the adoption and approval of this Agreement.

(b) The holders of a disproportionate number, in the judgment of the Board of Directors of Santa Anita, of shares of Santa Anita Common Stock shall not have exercised dissenters' rights under California law.

(c) Santa Anita shall have received from the Internal Revenue Service a ruling, in form and substance satisfactory to Santa Anita, to the effect that:

(i) rent to be received by Realty from LATC for the lease of the Santa Anita Park racetrack qualifies as rent from real property within the meaning of Section 856 of the Code; and

(ii) rent to be received by Realty with respect to commercial real estate developed by SDC will qualify as rent within the meaning of Section 856 of the Code.

(d) Santa Anita, Realty and Operating Company shall have obtained all orders, consents or approvals, governmental or otherwise, necessary to permit them to perform this Agreement in accordance with its terms, except for such consents with regard to such agreements and arrangements which are not in the aggregate material to the parties.

(e) Robert H. Grant, Richard L. Owen, Santa Anita, Realty and Operating Company shall have entered into the agreement described in Section 1.8 hereof.

ARTICLE FIVE

Termination and Amendment

5.1 Notwithstanding the approval of this Agreement by the directors and shareholders of Santa Anita, Realty and Operating Company, this Agreement may be terminated before or after such approval:

(a) by the mutual consent of the boards of directors of Santa Anita, Realty and Operating Company; or

(b) by the board of directors of any of Santa Anita, Realty or Operating Company if one or more of the conditions specified in Article Four shall not have been fulfilled and shall have become incapable of fulfillment.

5.2 The terms and conditions of this Agreement may be amended at any time before or after shareholder approval by the boards of directors of each corporation; provided that any amendment affecting the number of shares of Realty Common Stock and Operating Company Common Shares to be received in the Reorganization shall not be effective without shareholder approval.

ARTICLE SIX

Effective Time

6.1 After adoption and approval of the Merger Agreement in accordance with the requirements of applicable law and upon satisfaction of each of the conditions set forth in this Agreement (unless waived in accordance herewith) and in the absence of termination of this Agreement, appropriate documents shall be submitted for filing with the Secretaries of State of the States of California and Delaware. The date and time of filing of the Merger Agreement with the Secretaries of State of the States of California and Delaware is referred to in this Agreement as the "Effective Time."

ARTICLE SEVEN

Miscellaneous

7.1 Any of the terms or conditions of this Agreement which may be waived, may be waived in writing at any time by any party hereto which is, or the shareholders of which are, entitled to the benefit thereof by action taken or authorized by the board of directors of such party, or without such further authorization by the president or a vice president of Santa Anita, Realty or Operating Company, or any of such terms or conditions may be amended or modified in whole or in part at any time, to the extent authorized by applicable law, by an agreement in writing, executed in the same manner as this Agreement, after authorization to do so by the boards of directors of the parties hereto; provided, however, that no such waiver, amendment or modification shall have a materially adverse effect on the benefits intended under this Agreement to the shareholders of Santa Anita, Realty or Operating Company.

7.2 Expenses incident to the consummation of the transactions contemplated hereby shall be divided equally between Realty and Operating Company.

7.3 This Agreement may be executed in any number of counterparts, each of which shall be an original, but such counterparts together shall constitute one and the same instrument. No right or interest in or under this Agreement may be assigned by any party.

IN WITNESS WHEREOF, the parties to this Agreement and Plan of Reorganization pursuant to the approval and authority duly granted in the resolutions adopted by their respective boards of directors, or by ratification thereof, have caused these presents to be executed by the President or a Vice President and the Secretary or an Assistant Secretary of each party hereto.

SANTA ANITA CONSOLIDATED, INC.

By   ROBERT P. STRUB
_____
                                        President

and   ROYCE B. McKINLEY
_____
                                Assistant Secretary

SANTA ANITA REALTY ENTERPRISES, INC.

By   ROBERT P. STRUB
_____
                                        President

and   GLENNON E. KING
_____
                                        Secretary

SANTA ANITA OPERATING COMPANY

By   ROBERT P. STRUB
_____
                                        President

and   GLENNON E. KING
_____
                                        Secretary

Tentative Time Schedule for Santa Anita's Reorganization

DEFINITIONS

Santa Anita	Santa Anita Consolidated, Inc.
SDC	Santa Anita Development Corporation
LATC	Los Angeles Turf Club
REIT	Real Estate Investment Trust (either Santa Anita or business trust)
Grant	Robert H. Grant Corporation
SAE	Santa Anita Enterprises
SEC	Securities and Exchange Commission
IRS	Internal Revenue Service
O'M&M	O'Melveny & Myers
Leventhal	Kenneth Leventhal & Company
PW	Paine, Webber, Jackson & Curtis, Incorporated

Source: Royce B. McKinley, President, Santa Anita Realty Enterprises, Inc. Reprinted with permission.

Date	Action to be Taken	Party Responsible
April 19	Santa Anita Board of Directors authorizes proceeding further	Santa Anita
April 23	Finalize and file ruling request with IRS	O'M&M
	Commence identification of assets to be retained by REIT and to be transferred to LATC	Santa Anita
	Commence compilation of definitive list of all loan agreements, partnership agreements, joint venture agreements and similar documents which affect assets to be held by REIT or to be transferred to LATC	Santa Anita
	Commence preparation of outline of rental and other terms of lease between REIT and LATC	Santa Anita
	Commence research regarding reporting obligations of REIT and LATC under Securities Exchange Act of 1934	O'M&M
	Commence research regarding use of double backed stock certificates	O'M&M
	Commence research regarding necessity of filing registration statement with respect to distribution of LATC stock to shareholders of Santa Anita	O'M&M
May 1	Commence preparation of asset management plan for REIT	PW
	Commence analysis of relationship between REIT and SDC	Santa Anita, Leventhal
	Commence analysis of impact of transaction on Santa Anita pension plan, thrift plan, outstanding employee stock options and stock options plans	Santa Anita, O'M&M
May 7	Complete identification of assets to be retained by REIT and to be transferred to LATC	Santa Anita
	Complete definitive list of all loan agreements, partnership agreements, joint venture agreements and similar documents which affect assets to be held by REIT or to be transferred to LATC	Santa Anita
	Complete research regarding reporting	

Date	Action to be Taken	Party Responsible
	obligations of REIT and LATC under Securities Exchange Act of 1934 and discuss with SEC	O'M&M
	Complete research regarding use of double backed stock certificates	O'M&M
	Complete research regarding necessity of filing registration statement with respect to distribution of LATC stock to shareholders of Santa Anita	O'M&M
	Commence review of leases regarding property to be transferred to or retained in REIT	Leventhal
May 14	Complete review of leases regarding property to be transferred to or retained in REIT	Leventhal
	Complete outline of terms of lease between REIT and LATC	Santa Anita
	Commence analysis status of SDC as independent contractor	O'M&M
May 21	Identify assets to be transferred to or retained in REIT (definitive list as of this date)	All hands
	Commence analysis of impact of technical terminations of SDC and SAE partnerships	Leventhal
	Commence analysis of ability of SDC to dividend assets to Santa Anita under California Corporations Code	O'M&M Leventhal
	Commence preparation of final projections	Santa Anita, Leventhal
	Commence analysis of transferability of SDC partnerships and real estate	O'M&M
	Commence analysis of assets to be transferred to REIT by LATC and Grant	O'M&M
	Commence review of all loan agreements, partnership agreements, joint venture agreements and other relevant documents of Santa Anita	O'M&M
	Commence analysis of value of dividend of LATC stock to shareholders of Santa Anita	PW

Date	Action to be Taken	Party Responsible
May 28	All hands comment on outline of terms of lease between REIT and LATC by this date	All hands
May 31	Complete analysis of relationship between REIT and SDC	Santa Anita, Leventhal
	Complete analysis of impact of transaction on Santa Anita pension plan and thrift plan	O'M&M Santa Anita
	Determine disposition of outstanding employee stock options and stock option plans by this date	O'M&M Santa Anita
	Complete analysis of status of SDC as independent contractor	O'M&M
June 4	Finalize terms of lease between REIT and LATC	All hands
	Finalize recommendations for asset management plan	PW
	Determine impact of technical termination of SDC and SAE partnerships by this date	Leventhal
	Determine whether sufficient surplus exists in SDC in order for it to dividend REIT assets to Santa Anita by this date	Santa Anita, O'M&M Leventhal
June 8	Determine whether partnership and real estate assets of SDC can be transferred	O'M&M
June 11	Delivery of financial projections to management of Santa Anita	Santa Anita, Leventhal, PW
	Distribute first draft of lease between REIT and LATC	O'M&M
June 15	Determine preferred method of disposal of certain Santa Anita stock held by Mr. R. H. Grant by this date	Santa Anita, Mr. Grant
	Telephone conference with IRS regarding status of ruling request	O'M&M
June 18	Complete analysis of assets to be distributed to REIT by LATC and Grant	O'M&M
	Review all loan agreements, partnership agreements, joint venture agreements, and other relevant documents of Santa Anita by this date	O'M&M

Date	Action to be Taken	Party Responsible
June 25	Determination of value of dividend of LATC stock to shareholders of Santa Anita by this date	PW
June 27	Board of Directors formally approves conversion of Santa Anita into REIT, subject to receipt of IRS ruling	Santa Anita
June 30	Finalize lease between REIT and LATC by this date	All hands
July 9	Commence drafting proxy material	O'M&M
	Commence drafting documents to effectuate consolidation of Santa Anita subsidiaries into LATC	O'M&M
	Commence Blue Sky survey	O'M&M
July 15	Final agreement reached regarding disposition of Mr. Grant's stock	Santa Anita, Mr. Grant
August 24	Audit of Santa Anita's consolidated financial statements completed by this date	Leventhal
	Commence drafting of pro forma financial statements for proxy statement	Santa Anita, Leventhal
September 14	File Preliminary Proxy Material with SEC	Santa Anita, O'M&M
September 28	Receive IRS ruling request by this date	O'M&M
October 22	Receive comments on proxy material from SEC	All hands
October 31	Mail proxy material to shareholders	Santa Anita
December 4	Hold shareholders meeting	Santa Anita
	Commence preparation of closing documents	O'M&M
December 6	Complete disposition of Mr. Grant's stock	All hands
December 28	Closing	All hands
Thereafter	Prepare and file appropriate reports and other documents with SEC under Securities Exchange Act of 1934	Santa Anita, O'M&M

Index

About the Authors

RONALD J. KUDLA is Associate Professor of Finance in the College of Business Administration, Arizona State University. He is one of the authors of *Cases in Financial Management*. His articles have appeared in *The Academy of Management Journal*, *Journal of Business Finance and Accounting*, *Sloan Management Review*, and *Review of Business and Economic Research*.

THOMAS H. McINISH is Associate Professor of Finance in the College of Business Administration, the University of Texas at Arlington. His articles have appeared in *Journal of Business Research*, *Journal of Financial Research*, *Sloan Management Review*, and *Review of Business and Economic Research*.